Who Am I?

An In-Depth Guide to Empathic Communion

Lujan Matus

DISCLAIMER

ISBN-10: 1470063247
ISBN-13: 978-1470063245

WITH DEEPEST GRATITUDE

Thank you to Nyoman Suma and Kadek Gara
for your loving friendship during my time in Bali.
Thank you to all my students worldwide, for your enduring,
loving support throughout the years of our associations.
My beautiful wife, Mizpah, for your endless devotion.
I love you dearly.

Dedication

In loving memory of

Nyoman Suma

1973 – 2018

I love you Suma.

ACKNOWLEDGEMENTS

Editing, formatting, cover art and design layout

and back cover synopsis

by Naomi Jean.

Table of Contents

INTRODUCTION

After reading a letter Lujan had written following a post-death visitation from his father, I found myself looking at life with new eyes. The feeling reminded me of being sleep deprived and reaching a plateau of blessed equanimity; I was experiencing that very particular sensation of witnessing everything with the lucent gaze of one who doesn't have the resources to invest precious energy in the superfluous.

In this relaxed state, aversions and attractions, persona and identity, opinions and judgments, all fall by the wayside. One just is, and circumstances are simply as they are; bursting with the possibilities that present themselves within the new horizons that appear when we let go of what we were previously involved with.

What Lujan had revealed in that letter about illusions and the concept that life is composed of suffering was both disturbing and soothing at the same time. After reading it, I had the peculiar impression that a veil was continually being lifted, as quickly as it endlessly reformed itself.

I felt vulnerable but unconcerned, alert but empty, weary yet wiser, uplifted by a renewed sense of appreciation for the ephemeral world. What an unexpected relief to be freed of certainty through acknowledging the extent of my utter subjectivity. Noticing how deeply I had been affected, I wanted to share this revelation, to help release others from the spellbinding hypnotism of individual and collective bias.

It was clear that this was not something to be realized just once but a never-ending, moment-to-moment lesson to be learnt. I felt the simplicity of this information was so elegant that it could be immediately useful to just about anyone, and it thrilled me to imagine what a powerful effect it could have on many people's lives.

This gossamer-fine state of consciousness had been activated by a few words that in essence described how we are suffering an illusion. I had heard this before, and in countless ways! Yet somehow it hit me this time with an entirely new impact. I had gained a means to disengage my own conditioning simply by getting a glimpse at how deeply subjective our human perspective is and recognizing how much more is missed than is understood, at any given point in time. It was obvious right away that something was emerging that had to be shared.

The pervasive influence of bias in our lives is largely ignored or defended, at greater cost than we can afford to sustain. We need to completely revise the way we function, by actively applying adaptive perspectives that allow us to constantly recalibrate ourselves within the subtle dynamics of every moment we are confronted with. This fluid awareness will assist in illuminating the areas of our life that are not being noticed, so we can observe within our emptiness what is truly manifesting around us.

I will let you discover for yourself how the content of the initial text fractally unfolded into what has become the most surprising of Lujan's books so far. What poured out of his mouth and into these pages truly seemed to be writing itself at times. It was a delight to witness and had us listening with great interest as each chapter was revealed before our eyes.

I would like to take this opportunity to mention something about Lujan's character that may not necessarily be apparent to those who come across him through his writings, and that is his fundamental joyousness.

On numerous occasions I have witnessed a person who meets Lujan or hears his voice for the first time be taken aback by his good humor and abandoned laughter. Many are shocked to realize how gentle and lighthearted the person behind these teachings is in real life, for the gravity of his information has somehow led them to imagine a very serious figure. In fact, I also had an inaccurate impression prior to meeting Lujan, after hearing about him through a good friend's stories, which may be why I felt compelled to speak about that now.

What comes through Lujan is pure insight and direct life experience. He does not dwell upon this or consider himself important as a result of what he has been able to access, for it is not his identity but his purpose; to bring as many people as can listen into spheres of awareness that facilitate true growth. In this book he does a great job of conveying the intricacies of how we can all learn to access these innately human faculties within ourselves, bringing hope, clarity and heart to one's path.

Directly related to *Whisperings of the Dragon*, this book will also unlock new understandings and provide alternate perspectives on previous material. The profound and pragmatic truths that a person of power can acquire on the journey of life always reveal themselves anew as we grow into our availability to assimilate what we are ready for. To quote Lujan:

"To be somebody we must learn to be nobody, for only then do we arrive upon our sacred chance to be of service."

The world is calling us to hear it directly in our hearts. We need to remember how. We need to wake up and change accordingly. I sincerely hope it's not too late, for each and every one of us.

Naomi Jean.

AUTHOR'S NOTE

Many names have been ascribed to the light that gives substance to its own reflection via our awareness. We are fortunate as beings to behold the magnificence of such beauty as unfolds before our eyes. Yet it is this transfixed view that we have within a conflux of vibrations that hypnotizes us extensively.

Our belief systems contain us so neatly within the act of cognitive mirroring that we are subtly coaxed away from what is meant to be deeply recognized. The attunement of reality commissions our attention to attend to it meticulously, nesting us in a dualistic mechanism of separation toward the unknown.

The essence of void consciousness cannot be located via our prejudice, for as we covet the light through the bias of our perception we lose contact with the true source of our spirituality. This is the major issue that we are contending with, and the most jealously guarded secret that does not want to be discovered.

The engineered consciousness we have arrived upon via the states of awareness that we are confronted with within this three-dimensional illusion seems so substantially concrete within the exquisite complexity delivered. Our unwavering devotion to this continuous interaction creates a gravitational eddy that can be difficult to escape.

We are simultaneously subject, at this present time more than ever, to external influences that understand the applications of resonance focused upon our bioelectromagnetic field. This invisible interaction is only possible because we are all empathically inclined.

Our internal process of fractal osmosis automatically accommodates the entrance of light into the toroidal field of our DNA matrix, which switches genes on and off in response to frequential infiltration.

In most cases we have difficulty identifying the source point of these alterations for their application is automatically cloaked, beyond sensorial recognition by our ears and eyes. Yet, nevertheless, we are adjusted incrementally via the fact that our body naturally recalibrates itself to unseen and inaudible frequencies, with profound effects that we are only peripherally aware of.

Affecting us on many different layers of consciousness, this inevitably instigates an emotional response. Since we have been trained to thoroughly identify with our internal experience we won't, under many circumstances, look for an alternate origin to dysfunctional feelings that arise and possess us from within.

This leads to a mass weaponization of human awareness toward the simplicity of normal, day-to-day life, converting the beauty of our reality into a highly volatile dualism. Thus we find ourselves dealing with the pettiness of our circumstances instead of the essential complexities of what is happening beyond the microcosm of our confined view.

As a result, we lose our ability to see the holistic, macrocosmic effects surrounding us politically, socially and personally. We have been generationally coaxed to be ignorant of the fact that we are more powerful than what we really expect, and deeply conditioned not to truly believe in our own internal sovereignty.

A gradual erosion of one's internal ethics, for example through being politically correct because it is popular, is a training tool to distance us from our capacity to stand firm within our empathetic integrity. In other words, our ability to know what is really occurring and act accordingly.

What is manifesting before us always reveals only a fraction of this reality, and inherently reflects the hopes and dreams that surround this illusion. It is how we interpret the light within this hallucinatory state that will allow us to advance toward more refined frequencies to discover the intrinsic resonant fields that lie beyond the boundaries of what presents itself to us.

The real essence of creation in all its forms is by its very nature unknowable. Within this book, however, I will reveal how to establish contact with this mystery. As Yeshua once said, "Split the wood and lift the stone, you will find me there." It is within this place of no name that we discover the true essence of our self.

The book you are about to enter is complex within its simplicity and yet very easy to understand. But remember, the path of enlightenment is only a foot wide and a thousand miles deep, and as you personally travel towards your earnest realizations, your sincerity will reveal the magnitude of your responsibility as a human being.

I now welcome you into the most intimate journey that I have ever revealed of my life. As you discover me, it is my wish that you discover yourself simultaneously from your own empathic perspective.

Reflections

Looking through the corridors of my innermost feelings, I realize that what I was always searching for was love and affection, compassion and deep communion. My destiny as a human being has led me to seek these precious elixirs throughout my entire life.

In reality what I was truly looking for within others was what was continually available within myself. But, as we all know, what we possess within is challenged by the arduous journey we are confronted with. For if we look at it realistically, nobody's life is perfect, and this within itself is the greatest gift that has ever been bestowed upon us.

What I really mean by this is that we are all beset by challenges that test the original feelings that deeply abide within us, as beings that are perfect right from the very beginning. The gift of these trials and tribulations is to humble us upon our path.

Herewithin, I will relay the story of the last meeting I had with my father and how this event irreversibly impacted my life as a seer. My interaction in childhood with him was troubled and disturbingly disharmonious. We were never connected on the level of feeling and unfortunately remained estranged for the duration of his life. What I am to recount here is where our relationship truly begins, even though this new chapter began after his death.

I will attempt to convey everything that was imparted via his last intention, which was a gesture to resolve the power he was unable to obtain during his own lifetime. Via this unexpected contact he initiated a continuum of deep realization within me, and finally the true connection between father and son occurred.

As I personally acknowledge the impact of this meeting, I look back in my present moment at my life and realize that everything that is done can never really be undone. For in essence every circumstance that exists within our capacity to act has always woven within it subtle regrets. Growth always pinpoints what could have been and what should have been, even though it is just the way it is; and upon reflection that is all that matters.

Within that mirror image of our retrospective journey, subtleties that are meant to be seen are delivered to us. That which may have been overlooked arises to be reviewed and through this renewed viewpoint we discover where the power of our journey truly resides.

These fragments of my story will prompt memories of your own odyssey to lift the burden that besets the wisdom of your eyes, which is the fire of your own true realizations revealing the light upon your path.

It has been my fortune to be witness to the final passage of some significant people within my life, which were mere glimpses into a world that contains so many complexities yet to be unveiled. Within the scope of such visitations one can obtain luminous fragments that leave a feeling that conveys the true content of that momentary contact.

When you honestly look at this, isn't this what happens with a passer-by? Are we awake enough to be revealed to the vision that is our life witnessing itself? And is not the end moment the continuum that enlightens one's inner being as a consequence?

White Light

A full three months went by after my father died before he bestowed upon my life one of the most powerful gestures that one could ever experience.

I had been sleeping deeply and I awoke to a vision. What appeared in front of me was an extremely strong white light. Upon seeing it I went into an instant reviewal where I observed every aspect of my life. A kaleidoscope of memories was fractally passing me by at an incomprehensible speed.

As each scene made itself available to my internal visual faculty it appeared that the imagery ground to a halt to be observed introspectively for a timeless moment that seemed to encompass the entirety of that event, even if the experience itself had taken months or years to manifest.

I believe that we don't have much time left as sovereign entities to retrieve our ability to evolve towards our collective future via natural means. What I am referring to is our innate capacity to empathically communicate, which is the subject matter we will explore within these pages.

Whilst I was immersed within the all-encompassing frequency of that vast radiance I realized that an open vessel had been made available to my beingness, as many would say, at the behest or the grace of God. Witnessing this immeasurable luminosity I knew that those who use the common denomination, *God,* are referring to the revelatory effect this phenomenon has upon their consciousness when contact occurs.

Faced with this ubiquity, I immediately knew that there was no heaven and no hell. This was an absolute fable, just a story. It was part of our illusion; the myth of what we expect to discover when we die, which reveals the wish for a certain result to appear as a consequence of being at the threshold of those gates.

At that point of transition we are held within the reflection of our belief systems, and if we can't conjure the power of discernment at this crucial juncture, that manifestation becomes our total illusion.

Once we arrive, as far as our human awareness can determine, there is nothing but that white light. There is no past and there is no future. There is no retribution, and nothing to be recounted. There is only the fleeting reflection of what had taken place in your life, which bears no consequence upon that moment. The experience is extremely uplifting.

This all-encompassing vibration holds you within the essence of your higher self in terms of that heavenly frequency permeating your awareness until the moment that your consciousness dissolves into absolute unity. The white light has an incomparable capacity to instill devotion. You become totally immersed in the loving essence of its ubiquitous emanation.

There is a steadfastness delivered via that immersion that infuses you with heartfelt feelings of what you are meant to do and achieve as a being, one that is not encumbered by social restraints that beckon you to be absorbed in any form of negativity that may inhibit you from achieving your sovereign task; if you happen to return to your earthly continuum. This is what I absorbed when I gazed into its immensity.

Looking up into the white light, which encompassed everything yet was nowhere simultaneously, I saw a line or a horizon that split the scene into two distinct perceptions. What I was reflecting upon was a visual juxtaposition of both that luminosity and the earthbound reality that I was about to re-enter. Interlaced within that vision appeared a familiar voice that began to beckon my attention.

When I heard the words conveyed, immediately a deep realization of God consciousness came upon me. Now, although this is what arrived into my awareness, I wouldn't ascribe to it this small frame.

This was an indescribable ubiquity; a beautiful, intense being that harbored no memories. It is only there at the moment you realize it, and the sole consequence of that white light becoming available to you is through the mirroring of your own existence at the point of contact.

This boundless sentience spoke in multifaceted resonances, in a way that was very reassuring to my inner beingness, to establish the connectivity of the truth that was being portrayed. The structure of the information was simple yet held so many overtones of meaning.

Amongst the multiple layers being delivered, a message was conveyed that my journey is at a crossroads and that this was the gift of my father that was to be bestowed upon me.

The last part of his personal odyssey was to enter the light to recalibrate his beingness to the power of the man he could have been in his life. As he became that man, I felt the light turning around to gaze at me, even though there was nothing there to embody the gesture. It was just a frequency, yet it was simultaneously my father.

As he connected to me, the superimposed scene of the worldly construct I was in was glitching and flickering like a super-8 film. Then I heard my father's voice again, and as he spoke I felt a resounding power flow through me. So beautiful, so calm, so strong! His voice carried the fortitude and purity that he'd had the possibility to truly express while he was living. He was such a magnificent man who had fallen into confusion.

At that moment he gifted me with the only thing that mattered. It was an influx of realizations that were not spoken but arrived via his capacity to somehow remain stationary for the period of time necessary in order to come back and deliver me this one particular gesture.

That exchange recalibrated the insecurities I had absorbed as a child, reversing the emotional impoverishment that had previously been his legacy. It filled me with elation and reinstated a sense of wholeness and enrichment within our connection. He knew that this meant more to me than anything that I could ever express, and he was right.

This interaction was simultaneously happening in multiple layers of reality. It wasn't linear. The way it occurred was that as he was communicating to me, he slowly emerged from the light to finally appear as the man he was before he died; the man I used to know as a very powerful forty-year-old individual. As he conveyed the deep truths of our circumstances, I was totally held by the illusion that was being propagated.

In an instant, the light suddenly disappeared and there I was with my father descending into the realm of man, entering the three-dimensional confusion that is our collective illusion.

He was still very robust as he emerged, but somehow lost some of his purity or the command of his being upon arrival in this alternate realm. I noticed that there was something in his field of perception that couldn't sustain the energetic integrity that had expressed itself when he had first appeared.

Plummeting into the world, we ended up in a moving car. We were diving into the illusion of our symbiotic vision. My father was driving very erratically, and all of a sudden we were enveloped by a swarm of giant mosquitoes.

At the time that this dream vision occurred, my wife and I were living in Malaysia on an island called Langkawi. The man who took us shopping there drove like a maniac. When it rains in that region it is very dangerous on the roads and he actually took pleasure in trying to evoke feelings of fear. I attempted to ignore this but was always reminding him to slow down, especially as the type of van he drove had a reputation for tipping very easily.

He also often had dozens of mosquitoes in his car, which alarmed me greatly, as the last time I was living in Asia I contracted Dengue Fever and had almost died as a consequence of being bitten.

In the vision with my father the inordinately large mosquitoes were hitting our windshield and a few of them came inside. I started smacking them furiously, trying to kill as many as possible when I suddenly came out of it and said:

“FUCK! This is my illusion!”

The mosquitoes were my illusion! At that moment I realized everything all at once. I wildly looked up to my father and he said to me, “You suffered my illusion and I suffered yours.” Upon this affirmation, white light suddenly engulfed us both, and I awoke from the vision.

Life is Suffering

My father's presentation upon his departure delivered a magnificent awakening. That visionary experience brought me into a very deep understanding of realizing that everything is hidden in plain sight. All elements are available for our discernment, always in front of us, and we are forever contending with that illusion.

But can we see that what we have noticed may be - or even definitely is - a distraction that has given itself validity through our need to confirm that we are right about what we realize? Can we overcome our dissonance, our bias?

The inability to recognize what is meant to be deeply understood brings life into a sphere of the illusion of suffering, which is an extremely complex labyrinth that presents never-ending eddies that verify themselves as our certainty; within an endless narcissistic loop.

Maya[i] is a fickle mistress that doesn't want to reveal what is hidden, for her delight is in her capacity to manifest the internal emulation within us all that life is suffering. What occurred with my father gave me the impetus to commit to clarifying the mechanisms of this universal lie that has been awarded the mantle of truth.

This Machiavellian deceit pales in comparison to an empathic path, where one is subject to what one is meant to see, not what we have been told we need to know within the restrictive boundaries of an engineered consciousness. The illusion of

[i] Maya is a Sanskrit word with multifaceted meaning. Amongst those, the measurer of Cosmic illusion; The power in creation by which limitations and divisions seem to exist in the Oneness that is true reality.

suffering cannot be compared to our true destiny as intuitive beings.

The well-worn adage assures us: Life is suffering. This is how it works. For sure we can say it, for sure we can feel it, and in actuality we really experience it. We have been covertly manipulated not to be totally aware, and it is this lie that reveals itself as our collective truth.

Everybody experiences their joys and their sadness, and the downfall of our joy is to descend from the frequency of that vibration into an alternate resonance that doesn't yield as much pleasure.

We identify a point of change where we know that we are suffering, and we miss desperately what was there before when we find ourselves contained within something that doesn't seem to be as embracing or supportive.

As Buddha said: Life is suffering. You suffer the illusion of another as they suffer their illusion of you. Yet you can never really tell whether they understand the illusion that you are suffering. And quite frankly you know you don't fully understand what they are enduring either, and this realization will always be brought about by humbly accepting what cannot be known.

So life is suffering. It is only when you gently withhold your assumption that it becomes clear that to be of service is to understand what really can't be understood. This within itself is a form of waiting.

Within the clear atmosphere where your fortitude abides, you cannot inject anything other than what you momentarily recognize, even if the realization is simply that you must wait.

From this perspective, time presses upon your eternal present moments to allow you to acknowledge what needs to be patiently waited upon. We cannot assume that we know what we know, for the assumption itself is an illusion, and that bias propagates suffering from the perspective of its own subjectivity.

The content of someone's delivery denotes the suffering of that person who understands that moment in time, in terms of their own receptivity of that frequency which has arisen. So we all endure the collective illusion. And that is why life is suffering.

If you understand that the illusion is what you are meant

to suffer then you must move on to the next vital element of discovery, which is to become lovingly available to your circumstances. To be of service is to alleviate the illusion of somebody else's suffering.

You see your circumstances. You don't judge them. You activate your ability to forget what you think you know so that it doesn't bind you internally within that connection to unnecessary emotion, which ultimately leads to the very bias that is attempting to suffer its own illusion upon you.

Allowing that event to be placed over burning embers as if you were water turning into mist, you then rain down upon your environment as a refreshing moment that will only yield the chance of renewal. This is how you become available without interfering.

For it is *inaction* that you are performing, even though it may manifest as an external gesture of service, which doesn't betray the softness of your internal observance. Within this inaction you propagate your kindness, which is your compassion towards what you have seen. You give credible doubt to every single circumstance, for that is the only thing that will save you from judging.

Credible doubt means you acknowledge what you see but don't believe it to such a degree that it becomes your limitation and your vehicle of suffering towards the circumstance. You allow it a quantum centimeter of chance not to be that way when you don't supply the energy to build a construct around what you assume, nor give yourself credit in terms of validating your opinion. You let go of your assumptions, and when they are dropped an alternate view may become obvious.

Then you may see reality in a different way, which puts you in the position of continually being in a state of service, instead of servicing your own self-righteousness, which may be an illusion in comparison to what is waiting to be seen.

Look at it this way. You service the credible illusions that you are experiencing, which you can't escape from. The freedom of knowing that they are credible illusions gives you the ability to be of service to others, which opens up the door of your internal eye to actually observe another human being's limitation in terms of what they do with your availability.

These principles of accessibility and inaccessibility will be examined in greater depth as we traverse these pages. For now, let's put our attention upon the axiom of service.

Being of service opens up the possibility to see the ingrained negative undercurrent and layered internal gravity of individuals hiding in plain sight. I believe that most people on the planet at this present moment in time are fed up with subterfuge.

Maintaining a false front is totally opposed to the living philosophy of an intuitive empath, and we are suffering extensively as a direct result of this acculturated artifice, which betrays our real nature. We really don't need to put up with this any more. Becoming of service is one of the key antidotes to this collective illness.

We must under all circumstances witness the illusion we are suffering and learn to distinguish the very subtle elements of insight that outline the path we must follow. This is a very complex discipline. If possible, give a voice to what you see, yet simultaneously consider that your seeing could be under the influence of a personal bias.

The act of service will instruct you on how to go beyond the sway of your own partialities, which will give you the ability to be a silent observer within the illusion you must contend with, and eventually deliver you to the art of neutrality.

Within the illusion, you must diminish your own capacity to be somebody, for in essence it is more prudent to be nobody. In other words, to be there but *not* be there simultaneously.

Humble steps taken never reveal the sound of their approach, and from this perspective nothing is hidden. Even though this is cryptic, when you establish a deep understanding of this living principle, you will realize that *not knowing* is more valuable than *knowing*.

We can all comprehend that to strive to be unbiased within our struggle is to exist in a state of cognitive dissonance. Harmonizing that discordance via the clarity of the fluctuating truths that stand very patiently behind every circumstance waiting to become an alternate view - which may never be spoken or even seen by another witness - is to be subject to the suffering of that illusion which you must be of service to.

Remember to watch carefully, yourself more than anything else. In essence this is to be of service to oneself. That is the reflection that my father imparted. He came from the purest position and expressed his illusion to such a superb degree that it woke me up to a deeper understanding of his projection suffering upon my reality.

Recently I was asked a question by a student of mine who read a draft of this book before it was completed. She wanted to know whether the realizations outlined here relate to the concept of not taking things personally. She asked if the key was to recognize that we suffer but know that it's only an illusion and is going to change.

I simply replied that this was partially true but we have to look at it from more than one vantage point, for this understanding is also making the suffering conform to another illusion, which is the expectation that things will change. So you perform this as an *inaction* and this in turn transforms your observation into a not-doing.

You know what you know but you recognize that you've got to shift everything you realize into the area of credible doubt, since you fully acknowledge that your opinion is limited, however multifaceted it may be. If I change, I incrementally relocate those realities that co-exist with and are affected by the pressure of my beingness.

We all must realize that in actuality there is no objective concreteness to determine an ultimate goal that corresponds with one's expectations. For our timelines will shift in concordance to the pressure applied, and this is all determined via the field of anti-matter that is eternally fluctuating in conjunction with our conscious input; which is that field gazing through the vibrations of our reflections, back into its own abyss.

No matter who we think we are, we are never that person. We are always the next being who arrives upon our circumstance, via their witnessing. That is the truest individual you will ever meet; the one you may encounter the next morning, who gazes upon the sunrise as they drink their tea by your side.

To genuinely be of service is to recognize that life is

composed of suffering. And what a magnificent symphony it is. Within this frequency love will abound. To give the best of yourself to every circumstance without background noise is the essence of our progression as spiritual beings.

Be aware that personal history may loom on the horizon as an incessant resonance, and may be emphasized through the excessive familiarity of others. Cognitive loops will confirm that you are who that narrative says you may be. Our perceptual viewpoint can be dramatically thrown off-kilter via the subtle infusion of these repetitive installations.

Know that you may encounter circumstances that can never be resolved, and if you are faced with this eventuality, it is better to withdraw. In cases where you can't leave you just have to bear your destiny, for in actuality in some situations there isn't a choice and resolution may not be a possibility.

Remember upon this burden that the ultimate solution is to become of service. Then suffering becomes filled with purpose. Service burns all forms of retribution. But again, it is not always necessary to endure circumstances that are unbearable. Being of service must be balanced by discernment; there is no place for martyrdom. A bird cannot fly with only one wing.

I've written extensively in *The Art of Stalking Parallel Perception* and *Whisperings of the Dragon* about the situations that we all go through as sentient beings in our childhood. Maturing into a more complex, socially conditioned person who has the capacity to integrate, we find that assimilation causes the purity of youth to be consumed within the arbitrary demands of the social labyrinth.

When parents push upon the burgeoning consciousness of their child their unreasonable reasoning, the illusion of their suffering becomes that small being's distortion. This is a clear illustration of our collective suffering.

At the moment we can't recognize the resources at our very fingertips - the capacity to allow that child to grow into the joyful and enlightened perspective that there are no limitations, only what we can do for one another within the premise of pure service.

The empathic view is that:

Life is suffering.

Suffering demands service.

To be of service is to live with purpose.

And purpose is beautiful. It brings elation. It brings courage. It allows people to love you, and you fall in love with life as a result of your selfless and wholehearted engagement.

The Path of an Empath

To give a personal insight into our journey as empaths from multiple perspectives, I will relate a story that reveals the mechanisms of how beings of different phylums can communicate between each other, across the immense abyss that presents itself through the alternate conscious states that harbor unique, individual intelligences.

The most difficult thing to understand is the response in terms of the feedback loop that occurs through the echoes of visual, auditory, and feeling perspectives, which then lead to absolute understandings through the intuitive empath's insight, or *seeing*.

One has to take into consideration at this point that every human being who possesses the cognitive ability to represent what they have discovered on their journey can and will be altered via their respective bias at any given moment.

Your understanding upon the word *bias* must be comprehended very gently. In essence, bias can lead one to a state of cognitive dissonance, which must beckon the seer to let go of everything they know upon that moment, so as to see how the innumerable aspects of our attention will always be tilted toward the new moment that we arrive upon, which is continually escaping us.

After retrospectively discovering the event that has been witnessed, the seer's internal realizations must be renewed via the fact that an empathic absorption is never dictated by bias, and alternatively is always swayed by the new depths and horizons of the next circumstance coming upon them.

This is a warning to the perceiver who reads this material. Nothing is concrete, or absolute. If it becomes this way, dogma will dictate and human awareness will be thrown into reasonable premises instead of remaining receptive to the subtleties of innumerable changes perpetually arriving upon the moment.

I am continually subject to the truth of my present continuum, which not only illustrates but also allows me to speak of experiences that come upon me so as to further expand upon insight through an empathic view. I can only faithfully relate what occurs right in front of me, right now. Hopefully these accounts will be helpful to shed light upon how we are meant to evolve as light beings on this planet.

At the time of writing this book I was living in Bali, and a certain alignment occurred in terms of the information I am relaying, which synchronistically arrived while transcribing this manuscript.

What transpired will demonstrate the only way I can proceed as an empath, seeing through the veils presenting themselves at every instant. I don't particularly like the word *seeing*, since it has overtones that can mislead via the expectations of the perceiver.

My main objective is to establish the most profound

understanding in terms of how we receive information, so that we don't become subject to over-connoted explanations, but interact elegantly with the dynamics of our ever-changing circumstances that challenge us to commune faithfully. From even the very simplest viewpoint the deepest realizations can arrive upon the altar of one's heart.

This first story that I will portray has to do with a water spirit and how it injected itself into the lives of the people who lived in one particular house on this property. Its input was mischievous and evoked fear, since the way it made itself available was disturbing, and on some occasions frightening.

The initial information I was given about this spirit was that it had the ability to hide things of value. I heard of this only after I had relayed a mysterious event that had occurred with my wife and myself in the villa we were staying in to the manager of the property.

I told him that when we got home we went upstairs to the bedroom and put my wife's handbag down on the couch. It contained our passports and all of our other important documents, including credit cards.

When we decided to sit down and relax, I asked my wife, "Where is your bag?" We both looked towards the couch and it had disappeared. It wasn't there.

We searched the house in a panic, wondering where the hell it had gone. This was very unsettling to me because I am so acutely aware of our valuables in third world countries. After ten minutes of frantic searching, we found the bag right in the spot we had left it.

The first thing that the manager relayed to us after we had retrieved our belongings was that the house has a mysterious spirit in it that hides things. In fact, my wife's handbag is black and the couch is dark blue. What became obvious to us is that the spirit had lain its form down upon our valuables and made them disappear. We realized this after we were told one of the many stories about what had occurred in this house.

The couple living here previously kept their passports in the safe downstairs. The passports were black and the wallet in which they had their many important documents was the same color.

Before they were leaving to go to the airport for their international flight, they looked into the safe to retrieve their valuables and they were nowhere to be found. At this point they rushed to the Balinese manager and said, "We can't leave! Our property has been stolen."

Remember that the two of us were also searching for my wife's bag in the exact place we had put it. The previous tenants had done the same thing, looking in the safe. When the Balinese manager came down to check whether the contents were still inside, to the couple's surprise their belongings were right there where they had left them.

Here it is imperative to understand that this interaction inspired fear and dread in many people, and yet this was the only way the water spirit was able to convey its presence. We all must attempt to comprehend that the state of cognitive dissonance that we can be subject to in such circumstances exposes the faulty mechanisms of our perceptions in terms of our bias.

The embedded feelings that arise within in response to

unusual occurrences that traverse species-based and cultural affiliations reveal an inability to be situationally attuned with an alternate phylum. In this case, there was simply no other way for communication to occur without this being making itself available via these strange gestures.

The way that the Balinese deal with these innumerable complex circumstances is to appease such entities by performing ritual offerings so as to regulate their influence through the auspices of giving and receiving. But there is another way to proceed, and this is how it happened for me.

Every morning, I meditate for one hour. I awaken at five-o-clock, and in this house I have to go downstairs to begin my practice. Designed as an open-air environment, once you are on the ground floor you are inside and outside simultaneously. In the front yard there is a tree that has red flowers, and a toad lives under this beautiful plant.

The gardener, Gara, had told me about this toad. He said no matter what he had done, in terms of picking it up and throwing it over the fence and into the fields, this being always returned, to his utter dismay. He also relayed that at one time some children who were playing in the front garden with sticks had inadvertently broken the toad's back leg.

As a result, when it returned Gara always knew that it was the same one because of the visible injury. He only told me this story because I had thrown the toad on one occasion over the high fence into the field, as it was always defecating amongst the red flowers that I was cleaning up every morning.

I felt it was enough that I had to deal with the flowers and was concerned about catching parasites from the stool, as I sometimes picked up the red flowers and accidentally put my fingers on it. So I was also aware of the toad having a back leg that had healed in a crooked shape, which clearly identified it.

One morning as I came down to meditate, the sunlight was just beginning to illuminate the garden. It wasn't exactly semi-darkness and it wasn't quite dawn yet either. What I am to tell you now is the absolute truth, and will illustrate how I function as an empath in terms of obtaining information from even the most minute glimpse at my circumstances.

As I ventured downstairs and towards the kitchen, I turned on the lights and glanced up at the tree which possesses the red flowers that Gara and I have to clean studiously every morning so as to allow the day to proceed without the mess from the night before. This is an act of cleansing, of devoting oneself to the work, which becomes a gesture of service to the property itself.

On various occasions we would say to one another: Who is going to win, you or the tree? We both know this magical entity will always triumph, for its capacity to live beyond the lifetime of men has already been established.

In the tranquility of those early morning hours, glancing up to the trunk of the tree, I observed what looked like a black flag hanging in mid-air, about thirteen or fourteen feet from the ground. The circumference of the shape was around six by four feet and it wavered like black, rippling water before my eyes.

Conveying this vision to you, I must clarify that I only saw it for a split second. This was enough time for it to transmit from its phylum to mine a certain amount of information, and I grasped it all in that one instant.

Wordlessly, the presence transmitted to me that it was a water spirit. It had the power to communicate at that particular moment through its impressions that travelled through my eyes, into the depths of my heart, and bounced back to my ears as memories of something that had been spoken, yet nothing was said. In that instant it showed me its origin.

It was an entity from the river that flowed nearby, about a thousand yards from the house itself. It was able to convey this information to me because it had been raining hard the day before, and I myself had been absorbing the sound of the swollen river for ten or fifteen minutes during my early morning meditation. Its tumultuous white water rapids were singing loudly and had drawn my attention.

I went back to the memory of listening to the river's deluge. It had been so pronounced that I became transfixed by it's murmuring. This state of communion I found myself in with the river gave the spirit the power to transmit its message to me.

You must realize that I didn't do this on purpose. It was all randomly synchronistic and the sound of the water was an unwitting vehicle that the river spirit could traverse upon to convey its message to me.

Its story was that it loved the tree and would often possess the toad, traveling within its body and looking through its eyes to convey its presence within the vicinity of the red flowers that had fallen to the ground. I knew this immediately and irrefutably to be the truth, because before I had thrown the toad over the fence I noticed it looking at me with a strange gaze of knowing, which kind of disturbed me at that moment. It must have disturbed my friend Gara as well, since he had also wished to extricate this odd presence from the garden.

It was apparent that the spirit had been trying to communicate with us through the medium of the toad's eyes. Unfortunately it did not succeed because we both felt very strange about this bizarre creature, which we knew had returned from where it was obviously impossible for it to make its way back from. Within this explanation is all the communication that I arrived upon via one single momentary glimpse at this spirit.

At that point I knew I didn't want any more mischievous

behavior from this entity, so I went and picked some frangipani flowers, along with some incense and chili, as an offering that had two parts.

The flower and the incense would draw the spirit to the red flowered tree, and the chili would convey a message for it to curb its mischief. This offering was placed about six feet high amongst the branches, approximately where I had seen the entity appear. The communication was that it was welcome but not permitted to cause trouble any more.

I discovered the next day that Gara had also planted a chili shrub in the garden to repel the water spirit, two years earlier. The difference between the Balinese ritual and what I did is that they place their offering of incense, flowers and chili on the ground by the trunk, whereas I put mine halfway up the trunk in the midst of the leaves.

To my utter and total surprise, after I made this offering if anybody approached the house whilst we were away traveling the spirit would walk around upstairs, stomping like a heavy man on the floor and opening and closing cupboard doors in a loud slamming fashion to frighten the cleaners or the so-called intruders away, as I was told when I returned.

In essence, the water entity felt at home and then decided to be my protector instead of an annoying presence. I was informed when I arrived back home that a workman who had come over to fix a kitchen cupboard downstairs had run out frantically telling the manager: There is a ghost in Lujan's house! I was laughing when I said to the manager, "Don't worry, it's just my security guard."

Here I must mention that the distinction between a spirit and a ghost is quite defined. This was definitely a water spirit that was black in appearance, whereas a ghost can be connected to a cultural or family ancestor or a disembodied human being that has lost its way. They usually manifest as completely white.

After those incidents, I gently conveyed to the entity through my internal feelings to stop all of its territorial activities, and again, to my surprise, it desisted completely.

This is one of my first installments to explain how an empath communicates. Always information enters through the eyes, traveling to the heart, which gives the perceiver the power to speak of the story, or insights, via listening to what they can't hear and thereby inadvertently obtaining what seems to be unobtainable.

As you can see, this story is an enigma. Such an event can only arrive upon the simplicity of one's heart path; one's opening rapture to that which presents itself. The world unfolds to the humble gaze of a seer; which is the face of Buddha looking down with eyes half closed, totally in awe of that which is arising within as a true recapitulation of the position that he is subject to, via his service to the complexity that avails itself to his simple devotion.

In essence this is an insight into how an empath gathers information through collecting nothing yet being subject to the influx of sensory data that arrives upon their humble journey of service. It is merely a glimpse into the mysterious world of a universal participant whose destiny is unfolding within these extraordinary exchanges.

The first secret of an empath is the connection of their eyes to the sovereign majesty of one's centralized chakra. The voice of their emerging feelings reveals the truth of their heart, and at this point the ears recognize those inaudible scriptures. In other words, we receive another within those precious chambers.

We enter the world when we first take a breath. Within the quietude of our breathing, if we gently listen to that which can't be heard, we arrive upon our silence. Here we are contained, and yet have enough room to welcome another within. In this case it was a river spirit.

THE RECEPTIVE HEART

The only way to escape the eternal knot of *life is suffering,* is to realize that you must wait for the eruption of your heart to actually rise to the occasion with a natural urge to give of itself, in true response to the circumstance that you are witnessing.

The worldly paradigm at the moment is: *I want what I want, and I expect it to be given to me, otherwise there will be trouble.* This expectation and sense of entitlement that has been collectively cultivated is the opposite of what is outlined above.

In the world that we live in, there is a gridlock of consciousness surrounding money that amounts to slavery. The status that income gives to each individual creates a caste system revolving around economics that has forcibly defined our reality through its nefarious application.

The general consensus that people arrive upon within this corrupt mechanism is that they must earn their money and put it in the bank to try and save as much as they can. Within this cycle of relentless occupation, one's life force is depleted within the lie of the program: Work hard to accumulate enough resources to feel secure.

This is unadulterated slavery. Even the terminology used reflects the entrapment. We put our money in the *safe*, but nobody feels safe. The idea of saving one's income has a negative transformative effect upon an individual's consciousness.

Introspectively, everybody that is involved in the paradigm of saving paper will be presented with the long-term effects of the corruption of enslavement. It causes a form of greed and an inherent resistance to giving as a result of the time spent in the toil of one's life.

A parent may give to a son or a daughter more than they

can afford in comparison to what they have earned; yet when it comes to sharing resources with someone outside of the family unit there is resistance, since no relationship of trust or love has been formed, thanks to the divisive system we have been brought up in.

Instead of extending generosity where it is needed, most people will say to themselves, "Who will look after me if I give away my money to you?" Here is where the fear of not having what one needs blocks the heart from its true journey.

An empathic perspective, which is being overlooked on the planet at the moment, is that I want to fulfill your desires, your needs. I want you to feel safe and loved and cared for, because I have no fear of giving. For once my resources are depleted, there is another empath watching my circumstances, knowing that what must be done will be their capacity to fulfill my needs.

This phenomenon of empathic giving is a continual exchange, fractally moving within the confines and the limitless boundaries of all human interaction. It is the opposite of the paradigm we are subject to right now, which is the reason I am writing this book.

With the small, delicate gestures that I am to portray within the circumstances I am confronted with here in Bali, you will see, as I am seeing, that a crucial threshold has been reached and we are moving very subtly towards *the rapture*: the golden age that is our true heritage as intuitive empaths.

One of the primary mechanisms that levered us away from our inherent capacity to communicate empathically was set in motion when gold was changed to paper, thousands of years ago.

Just imagine that a merchant had ten thousand dollars worth of gold in his safe, and his greed was beyond anything you could conceive of. He calculated, very carefully, that he could loan out the ten thousand dollars worth of gold to many different individuals.

When his resources were depleted and he couldn't loan any more because that's all he owned, he then decided to lie to his new prospective customers, telling them that he had more gold than he really did. This is how this very deeply embedded duplicity began.

Not only did the merchant realize that he could do this, he also calculated that he could charge more interest than was fair for the money he had lent, and this eventually developed into the mafia-style taxation that we see all over the world at the moment. Here is where our freedom of giving became our fear of losing our resources, via the greed of our landlords and moneylenders.

Although this is a highly compressed and non-comprehensive explanation of this vast subject matter, I don't really wish to linger too long in such negativity. However, the truth of our worldwide situation is that we are staring down the barrel of a very strange gun.

All I'm wishing to portray is that almost every individual on this planet has been targeted and coercively programmed to accept absolutely unreasonable exchanges for their life force to be exhausted within. So let's turn our awareness towards the most beautiful and loving gestures that we are meant to be engaged within, and one by one realize that there is something terribly wrong on this planet at the moment.

The way to alleviate this collective binding, this Luciferian agenda, is to love so completely in those circumstances that allow us to, even within the limiting conditions that require our total attention within life's toil.

Here, within our heart of hearts, we will awaken one by one, until the critical mass of consciousness goes beyond the one percent. Exponential change will then occur so rapidly that we will be thrust forward into our new, loving paradigm with a momentum that will leave behind all our habitual behaviors in the wake of our progression.

Now I will return to the beauty of my personal circumstances, to give an example of what is meant to be instead of what has been studiously calculated towards us as a humanity: the lie that does not allow us to see the nightmare of what we have accepted as a result of the blinding force of that relentless program whispering to us: *That's life.*

Where I am now, in Bali, there are two beautiful men who I have become friends with. One is Gara, who you have already met, and the other is Suma, the manager of our property. The three of us have made a very powerful connection that we are all aware of simultaneously.

To comprehend how the intuitive sense of an empath operates within the human psyche, we have to look at the feelings that arise in terms of other people's desires becoming our wish to give.

What comes upon us may not make sense at the time, yet the world beckons the empath's eyes to look upon a particular item that silently alerts you to its presence – as it happened in the story I am to tell – and this compels the seer to act upon the decision of their internal impulses that subtly press upon their heart from the world at large.

An empath acknowledges what knocks upon their being and acts instinctively toward that transmission from an alternate phylum that is lovingly observing us. This is the God consciousness that emerges from the realm of antimatter, which we are continually being born into through its ethereal influence upon us.

This in actuality was our original heritage before the all-encumbering social program established dominance as an obligate parasite[ii], displaying characteristics not too dissimilar to those of the cuckoo, who takes over another bird's nest by placing its own progeny amongst the eggs of an alternate species, to be raised by the host. When the cuckoo chick grows to be larger and more aggressive than the other baby birds, they cannot compete and almost invariably perish due to the untenable circumstances they are confronted with.

The insidious truth of the social program is that this parasitic mechanism is being applied to our own species, unbeknownst to the collective whole, by a very powerful fractional minority. Prior to this takeover, we all interacted very differently. Allow me now to illustrate an example of the natural, intuitive functioning of an earthling.

Yesterday, the four Balinese girls who clean our house

[ii] An obligate parasite is an organism whose life cycle cannot be completed without exploiting a suitable host.

came in to do their job. By virtue of the fact that I always keep the house immaculate, they don't have to do very much when they arrive. We always take this opportunity to scoot off into the master bedroom to sit down and talk and laugh together about the events that have occurred during the week.

This was a Wednesday, which is also the day I have my coconut water delivered. We were sitting in the room, laughing happily, when my body suddenly became alerted. I stood up as if there was somebody listening at the door, though not a sound had been heard.

The girls looked at me with wide-eyed concern, thinking that the owner was about to catch them relaxing and enjoying themselves with me for five minutes instead of working. I quickly opened up the door and there, standing in the lounge room, was the man who delivers the coconuts.

I welcomed him and asked, "How long were you waiting for us to come out of the room?" and he replied, "I didn't know you were there, I only just arrived."

This is how an empath operates. You don't know why you

stand up; you don't know why you go to the next room. Yet I found myself rising and greeting the deliveryman. I didn't congratulate myself for this. I just paid the man, thanked him, and put away the coconuts.

To further elucidate upon this subject I will now share with you the story of what happened over a five-day period between myself and my two friends, Gara and Suma.

My wife and I were coming home from having an early lunch, and we stopped off at a little store to buy a broom. As we did so, a man selling ceremonial knives drove by and smiled with delight at me. I smiled back, thinking nothing of it, and proceeded to head home. Unbeknownst to me, this was a pre-emptive event.

Three days later, I began to have a very strong feeling that Gara wanted a ceremonial knife for the Galungan festival that is celebrated here at this time of year. To my surprise, we once again crossed paths with the guy who sells knives on his little old motorbike. Strangely enough, we were shopping in the same store where we had bought a broom from previously.

I hailed him over to where we were standing so we could

look at the variety of knives he had in the box, which hung from his motorbike. To my disappointment I couldn't find the ceremonial knife that looked like a smaller version of a coconut cleaver. I was almost going to forget the whole thing when I noticed a long, machete-like knife that was about half the size of a normal one. It was in a nice brown leather sheaf and had a superbly crafted wooden handle.

We haggled for a bit, came to a satisfactory agreement about the price, and then waved him goodbye as he rode off into the small village, disappearing around the corner where the rice fields begin. I popped the knife in the back of my jeans and Mizpah and I jumped on our bike to ride home. When we arrived, Gara was there, waiting with a big smile on his face.

"Guess what we've got for you!" I said, and he strolled slowly towards us to find out. When he was close enough, I pulled out the gift and presented it to him. "This is for you, for Galungan," I told him.

He looked at me with great surprise and began to say, "I have been thinking about whether I can afford to buy one of these knives, for - " I cut him off abruptly and said, "Three days." He was visibly shocked and asked, "How did you know?"

We both smiled and Mizpah replied, "Good luck is coming upon you because you are such a good person." Gara grinned mischievously and asked me again, "How did you really know?"

I answered that it is because we have got such a strong heart connection, then gave him a hug, and said, "I hope you enjoy it." He very humbly thanked me and told me he would take it home to his village, Singaraja, and perform a ceremony of blessing upon it to prepare it for use.

This is an irrefutable example of how the internal receptivity of an empath manifests. I must issue another warning here about this intuitive process. One can never be in a state of self-congratulation about their abilities. What transpires in one's life must be humbly acknowledged only in terms of giving and receiving in kind. If it goes beyond the simplicity of pure exchange, the ability will simply vanish from the perceiver.

Being engaged within the symbiotic process of empathic interaction means you function with the desire to give, but you have no idea that it's something somebody else wants until you become totally familiar with that particular principle, which means you become of service.

When I obtained the ceremonial knife for Gara, I fulfilled his desire. It was my spontaneous wish that made me want to do it, but that was really his true need. If I say, "Aren't I so good, that I realized what he wanted," that will put me into a state of suffering, because I'm not the person I am portraying.

It is the humility that is speaking through my actions. It is only because I realize that I am nothing that I have the capacity to be somebody for him.

To be somebody you have to be nobody, and to be nobody gives you the ability to read the feelings of your brother's and your sister's desires within your own heart. This is the way that we are meant to function, as symbiotic empaths.

It has been attempted by many enlightened beings since time immemorial to re-inject this natural state of inner receptivity into humanity. This is why the Buddha said that life is suffering and then strove to clarify, through abstract means and direct example, how to proceed harmoniously into the subtle depths of the world by selflessly giving and humbly receiving.

To fully comprehend this beautiful living philosophy, we are going to attempt to retrospectively tilt our eyes to look upon the ancient principles of dharma, adharma, the path of the abyss, and a few key techniques that have been practiced for centuries - Mantras and Sutras - in a way that will open your view to new perspectives upon their application.

This information is so simple and direct that you will realize that what you may have been taught about these subjects was not only non-applicable in many cases, but not explained in a way to make them absolutely functional in everyday life.

When I revealed some of these techniques to my Indonesian friends who have been practicing such spiritual principles for their entire lives they said to me that I sound like a Balinese priest, for the new frame of reference opened up their devotional approach to a broader and more encompassing perspective.

I responded to their kind praise by saying that I am

nobody, and my friends looked at me with a playful glint in their eyes, saying, "Of course. You are nobody, Lujan."

One thing that is crucial to understand is that when you follow a path with heart or the dharma of emptiness, you are in a absolutely receptive state to other people's desires, or their true needs.

The obtaining of a ceremonial knife was my friend's heart's longing, for it is not only required for the traditional rituals but also attracts respect from the extended family, who can request to use it when he is away working in another village. So his true need becomes my desire to give to him, and then this gesture benefits many.

Let's now gently enter into one more story, which reveals from another point of view the symbiotic effect that empaths travel upon, which is accessed through the mechanisms of introspective silence beckoning one to proceed upon a path that only unveils itself after their steps have been taken.

This is the discipline of disciplines: not to look back and point at the impression that has been left by your feet and say,

"That was where I left my mark, come and look." True power resides in not knowing where the next step will be taken, for there lies one's irrefutable destiny, in humble service to that which has not yet revealed itself.

A couple of months ago, when we arrived in Bali, we rented a dirty old motorbike that rattled, coughed and spluttered as we rode along. It was a small scooter and to ride it I had to open my legs up like a frog in order to be able to steer it. I said to Mizpah, "This bike is kind of dangerous. We need to get something bigger."

I spoke to Suma, the manager of our property, and asked him whether it was possible to exchange it for another scooter that was not so old and rickety. The next day they delivered, to my dismay, a bike that was in even worse condition. This one had brakes that didn't work.

I said to my wife, "I really appreciate the bike we had before. I wish I never asked them to swap it. I think they are punishing me for not being satisfied."

On the day we got the second bike it was Suma's day off. I

told the owner of the villas what had happened, and to my surprise he directed an enormous outburst of anger on the telephone to the people who had rented the bike to me.

Within ten minutes they arrived to check what was wrong and brought me back the original bike. As I gently thanked them the owner was still in the middle of guilting them whilst I was trying to exit this untenable situation.

The next day when Suma came back to work I told him what had transpired and he said, "Lujan, I've got a great idea. How about you continue with the one month rental of this bike and when that is over, if you can pay me up front for the rest of the time you are going to be here, then I can buy a motorbike which will be safer for you to ride. I have some money saved already, so with the extra cash I can afford to get a brand new one."

I asked him if we could just get the money back from the people who were currently renting me the scooter, since it was only one day into this month's rental arrangement. He replied that they were friends of his and he didn't want to offend them by asking for a refund.

I understood immediately because village life can be very complicated when it comes to offending people. After I heard his explanation I didn't want to put him in that position, so I agreed to wait. Here is where we will enter into what began to occur between Suma and myself in terms of our intuitive connection.

On this day, Mizpah and I were going to have lunch at the Shady Shack, our favorite local restaurant where they make beautiful cooked and raw vegan meals. After we had eaten, I noticed somebody parking out front. They had a big motorbike, larger than the one Suma and I had discussed getting. I looked at Mizpah and said to her, "A bike like that would be a lot safer for us."

When we arrived home, I saw Suma waiting for us at the entrance of the office. He waved me in and said, "Lujan, I've got a better idea. Why don't we get a bigger bike?" and he brought out his smart phone to show me a picture. "It will only cost a little bit more." As he passed me the phone, I said to him, "I was just looking at this bike and said to Mizpah that it would be better for us. How did you know?"

He answered, "We are developing a heart connection." I looked up at him with a glint in my eye and said, "That is really true." I got off the motorbike to give him a hug and asked, "When are we going to do this?" "As soon as possible," he replied enthusiastically.

As the weeks went by, our connection grew stronger and stronger, and on one occasion I noticed that he had glaucoma in both of his eyes, especially the right one. It was so swollen and pronounced that it was pretty obvious he had serious problems.

I asked him what was wrong with his right eye and suggested he go see a doctor about the swelling, and also immediately change his diet to as raw as possible to facilitate the mechanisms of his own healing. "You are right," he said, "but I don't know what to do."

I told him to speak with Mizpah, so that she could advise him on how to proceed. He then elaborated on what had been happening with his eyes. One year prior to meeting me, he had an operation on his left eye to remove a cataract. The cataract in his right eye had been so severe that he was completely blind on that side. This concerned me greatly, for I had realized that when he looked at me I couldn't feel an absolute connection, and now I knew why.

I asked him how much it had cost to get the cataract removed. He told me that it was a few hundred dollars. I said to him, "Why don't I give you the money and you go get the other eye done?" He started crying and said, "Lujan, you are so kind."

A few days later, I went to his office to speak about our leaky roof. It was rainy season at the time and there was a broken tile where the water came in. As I approached him I realized that I should advise him that even if the operation costs a little bit more, I wanted him to get it done. I had already given him the first installment and a bit more wouldn't make any difference. I instructed him to go ahead regardless and do what he needed to do.

Suma said, "Lujan, you are a really strange man. So many times I am about to say something to you and out of nowhere you begin to discuss exactly what I want to speak about. This time it is way too strong for me to ignore. I have to tell you. I was discussing with my wife last night that maybe the price would be higher than it was a year ago."

"Well," I said, "When you are around good people, these strange things happen. And you are Balinese, you know about the intuitive connection. If it's there, it's there. If it's not, it's not." He smiled at me and said he would make an appointment for next week and ask his boss for time off to recover.

The week went by and Suma came back with the news that he had seen the doctor. He said that everything I had discussed with him about his eyes - both the glaucoma and the pterygium developing in his left eye that was affixed to a swollen blood vessel and would have to be removed - had been confirmed by the doctor. "How did you know all that?" he asked me, "Are you an eye doctor?"

"No," I replied, "but I have worked with doctors in the past and I never forget anything I have learnt. In this case though, I diagnosed you through the feelings that arrived in my body as I gazed upon you. That's how I knew what needed to be done. Everything you gaze at reflects itself back to you as tangible information that can be decoded."

"That's just unusual, Lujan," he said, "Even our priests can't do this.

"It's no big deal," I told him. "I am a simple man, governed by simple principles. I truly care about your situation, and this is how I access your world. It is the same way you accessed my world when you knew which motorbike to choose before I even mentioned it to you. You are doing exactly the same thing I am doing. You are the holy man, not me."

He looked at me with big smiling eyes and slapped my shoulder. "I do have one more thing to tell you though. The doctor said I need to fix everything in one session, and he has proposed a package for me. He told me he can't fix one eye and not the other. Because of this the price has gone up."

I asked him how much more and he said, "You don't want to know." "Of course I want to know." I assured him. "The doctor said it will cost four times the original amount, and it is critical to operate now, for both eyes are in danger of loss of sight. Even though the right eye is already completely blind, he told me that it can be repaired by removing the cataract and reducing the glaucoma.

"This needs to be done so that he can observe the retina properly, as it is under too much pressure at the moment from the swelling and could be irreversibly damaged and detach without our knowledge, since I can't actually see it happening. The left eye has a massive pterygium growing over the pupil with a huge blood vessel attached to it, and if this is not dealt with I will eventually become blind in that eye as well."

As he was explaining this, I was aware that the Pterygium is very painful, like having sand in your eyes when you blink. I said I would have to go and speak with Mizpah about the extra expense before I could confirm that we would be able to go ahead.

I discussed the whole situation with my wife, and she said, tearing, "If it was you, this would be nothing for us. He is such a beautiful person. We can't be in a state of financial fear or poverty consciousness."

"Yes, you are right," I said to her. "Even though this is our emergency money and it is meant to save us in an unforeseen circumstance, it will now be put towards saving his sight."

I gave my baby girl a big hug and said I would be back in five. I proceeded to go and speak with Suma, which took all of ten minutes. I handed him the extra money he needed and gave him the go-ahead. "Do what you need to do." He said, "Lujan, you are one in a million. You are like a god to me." "No, Suma," I said, "I am just your friend, and we are just caring for you, the same way we would care for ourselves."

After he hugged me, I said to him, "With this gift, there are no strings attached. I don't expect anything in return. Once this money enters your palm, it was never mine as far as I am concerned. Text me when your operation is finished so we can come and visit you."

To complete this account, we must go back to the day of the Galungan ceremony. I was at home, walking up the stairs, and as I reached the entrance of our bedroom I had to lean on the doorframe with the weight of all the realizations that were coming upon me at once.

Tears welled up, as I reflected upon the overwhelming

influx of feeling connected to a confluence of stories surrounding one unusual being, a female dog who lives here, named Larry.

This dog, who decided to make these villas her home, is very skinny and sick, since everybody is scared to feed her as the owner of the villas insists that she shouldn't be encouraged to be here. Every time we arrive home on the motorbike, she lifts her head gently and wags her tail to greet us. We could see in the first week of being here that she was terribly weak from not being fed.

We too had been ordered not to give her anything, and this was irrefutably wrong. I said to Mizpah, "What difference does it make to the owner if she is fed, or starving and suffering, if she is here anyway?" and Mizpah suggested that we could sneak her food when the owner is not around.

I began to realize, as we became familiar with the routine of the villas, that Suma and everybody else were also giving Larry small amounts of food to curb her suffering, but not enough for the owner to notice. That's when I decided to start feeding her properly on a daily basis to fatten her up, so that she could enjoy the rest of her life, for she was quite old.

As I was walking up the stairs, I was looking back in retrospect upon this circumstance with this harmless being who obviously had made a connection and wasn't going anywhere, and who needed to be loved.

The reason why I got upset about this situation is that the Balinese make a gesture towards their crown which represents honoring God, and a gesture to the third eye which honors the ancestors, and a gesture to their heart which represents the honoring of our brothers and sisters.

When I asked, "Is there a gesture to honor the animals?" Suma told me, "There is no blessing for this. You simply can't do that."

As I went through the memory of all the events, I realized that we were all honoring this being by individually feeding her. The most beautiful thing that I witnessed was on one occasion when I accompanied Suma while he gave her some of his rice. I was quite moved when I realized what he was doing. He laid the food down on a paper plate and stood there keeping her company within a reverent stillness until she was finished eating.

I noticed that she would look up gently at Suma and myself with obvious recognition of what he had done for her. There is no boundary, no limitation, in actuality, between species. As caretakers of this planet we just need to recognize the varying responses from each being and act accordingly.

On the day of the Galungan ceremony, when Suma came to the property to perform his blessings at the temple down by the river near our house, he had also found himself crying at the same time that I was having massive internal realizations standing on my stairwell.

When he finished, he came to the house and asked me, "Lujan, why was I crying during the ceremony? My wife was looking at me strangely, wondering what was going on." I said to him that this often happens to people when they are around me a lot. "This is your rapture. The lifting of our heart's to a higher dimension."

A few days later, Gara came back to the villas and he described a similar phenomenon that had been occurring for him simultaneously. He said to me, "Lujan, I was telling my family about what you did for me, and I started crying."

Love is a strange thing.

We were all experiencing the rapture at the same time. Each one of us had our own encounter with the feeling of the opening of our heart towards our diverse circumstances, which had nothing to do with the motorbike and nothing to do with the ceremonial knife.

Even though the dog was a catalyst for me, the praying at the temple for Suma, and the storytelling for Gara, these were just elements of initiation to induce our awareness to the hiddenness of this sacred being revealing itself to us simultaneously.

In a situation of this nature, if we can see beyond our present bias to realize the beauty of what is touching us at the most opportune moment that is available, we can recognize the absolute ubiquity, the essence of universal consciousness, within its fractal ability to connect our hearts as one. This is the most difficult thing for us to understand; that this beingness is reaching through and creating that rapture for us within simultaneity.

A threshold of absorption whispered its presence and as a

consequence our tears rained down upon our hearts, enlivening a newfound neural network of connectivity. Our synapses were firing as if a universe of light had come upon us within the microcosm of our inwardly gazing eye, joyfully witnessing that rapture.

As a human being, to fathom the enormity of this alternate view, one must let go of the ever-present filter that blinds us to what is occurring behind that subjective reality that is convincing us at every moment that *it* is the only thing that can be seen.

Look upon this from the perspective of my own internal eye, but be careful not to be caught within your own prejudice as I tell you this parable. A fallen angel, as it plummets, can only realize its descent while occupied within that falling. There are many abstract tales that have been told to help describe our dilemma over the millennia, and this is my humble contribution.

It is said that this angelic being, who is just a representation of our beingness falling from its own grace, was extricated from heaven via being blinded by its own light, thereby becoming subject to the fractal anomaly of separation that has been given the name *sin*.

This led the angel to believe that God was the protagonist behind that devastating blow of expulsion, which became that angelic being's suffering of the assumptions surrounding that illusion.

If we recognize the terms and conditions of bias, we will begin to understand that it is the fallen angel's destiny to experience its incapacity to assimilate the enormity of the ubiquity that has been given the name of God. The individuated consciousness only has the capacity to witness the fragment that sheds itself from the omnipresence.

As it is faced with its own journey and the limitations that occur within that framework, the being forgets its origin. The unfolding subjectivity, which is the understanding that blinds the angel via the process of its own descent, is the same thing that is happening to all human beings.

We are so occupied with the filter of distortion that is our story that it becomes virtually impossible to perceive an inanimate being that is neither black nor white, positive or negative, good or bad. Its phylum exists beyond the contradictions of duality.

We are led to see our own assumptions as a truth. Via the illusion of that suffering we lost contact. Can you see the veil that is the explanation that is toiling to be undone? Yet, this ever present being that touches us has no toil, and the continual knot of our lives does not even exist for that omnipresence. To give substance within the light is to degrade its purity.

The Trojan Horse

The time has come to have a more in-depth look at one of the many roots of the social program, to discover how our awareness as human beings has been shifted away from its essential beauty, and how to return.

The first thing that has to be recognized is that all of us, in terms of the collective consciousness of humanity, have been severely redirected into a state of being that has nothing to do with who we really are. How exactly does this happen?

This is an all-encompassing subject and I will endeavor to lever the most pertinent areas of information to the surface, to be examined by our feelings. Let's proceed down a practical path by focusing on a few basic truths.

By observing the eruption that occurs within the chest when one becomes aware, we see that there can be two points of arrival. The first is an empathic response, and the second is a socially engineered reflex that is constantly being redefined to align humanity in a way that keeps us occupied with all the things that really don't matter.

The stories of Suma and Gara very clearly outline the first manifestation: how feeling can be transformed into action based on insight, which is a mode of communication that instantaneously comes upon a human being to be reviewed and understood in its entirety within a matter of moments.

Traveling upon this impulse is how we all find the next port of call, which elegantly unveils itself via the internal mechanisms that reveal the collective inspiration, through many individuals acting upon one point simultaneously.

When feeling is changed and manipulated into another form of communication, which becomes emotional modes of relating using the vehicle of language, the second modality arises.

To comprehend this fundamental transformation, let's turn our attention to the subtext that is imposed upon our beingness via semantics, as corroborative points that anchor that dysfunctional emotion which has been given functional meaning in terms of our reflective understanding of it. This is going to be an anthropological study of our change of consciousness from one state to another, and how to change it back.

The first thing that manifests within human physiology is feeling. In the beginning there's nothing *but* feeling. And feeling can be reduced to a frequency or a vibration. But a vibration ends up being aware of itself, and this comes back to the same point: We are a mass of feeling. And within that convergence there are many different frequencies that sustain awareness in pockets of variance.

How do we get to the point to understand what pure feeling is? This is a very hard thing to discover, since feeling happened before we were able to realize who we really are, and before we learned how to translate the import of information into words, without the intervention of thought.

As you traverse these pages you will begin to realize how we have been coercively maneuvered away from an empathic view and into a limited human perspective in terms of being socially governed. Even if that misdirection is only a few points off north, it's enough to make rediscovery of ourselves virtually impossible to encounter.

We struggle to absorb true information, for the popular world strategy at the moment is to saturate people with a false perspective of reality that ensures that we are off-point. We are not completely present. We are constantly dealing with illusions and the lies of those false propagations.

You may say, "OK, I understand that we are feeling beings, but how does a person return to this origin and make a new start?"

The reason it is so challenging to arrive at that cognitive point is that the original position had nothing to do with deciding what you are going to do. You must realize that it is almost a different phylum altogether. Feeling doesn't have the same points of reference, or an interpretive, linguistic system, to actually describe what is happening to it. Insight is its vehicle of communion.

The confusion begins when somebody comes along to a child – a fully developed feeling being with no shields – and embeds their bias and distortions via everyday interaction.

This internally aware being that is so vulnerable is now subject to projected emotions which have got to do with the process of semantic programming within other peoples' consciousness attaching dysfunction to their communication.

Imagine, from your own vantage point right now, that you are a highly sensitive empathic being that is childlike, yet you are a physically mature adult. In the beginning it can only be understood this way.

Your sensitivities and vulnerabilities are your intelligence, via the fact that these modes of feeling can immediately calculate the formula necessary to see what needs to be known, through the vehicle of understanding that is the frequency of innocence.

These two points of reference must be gathered in terms of *then* and *now*. It is the *then* of empathic receptivity that has been manipulated into the *now* of distortion.

Your understanding may be reflecting upon *now* through the bias of the program that you have inherited, which has taken a position of authority over the capacity of *then*; which is the innocence that was inside an incapable physical body that housed the child you were.

It is a loop that is confounding, for we have forgotten what we are meant to remember. But what we are meant to recall cannot be known via an avenue of cognitive bias. This is how we are locked within the program, which has been described as the neuro-linguistic process of so-called *understanding*, which in essence is intelligent enough to forget the innocence.

There is the trap. We can't conceive of what's not meant to be thought about.

If I sit next to somebody and do not have an internal dialogue actively running, can I receive their thoughts as an intention? Yes I can. But it is the internal process of understanding this that can be confusing in the beginning. When you become aware of somebody else thinking about what is about to happen, is the realization yours or theirs?

One can never know until there is a corroborative point of understanding reached. In the burgeoning stages of becoming empathically aligned, to understand what you *can't know*, transparency has to be established as a basis of true communication.

If your thoughts become my intentions, then one loses their absolute privacy, and people do not want to admit that this can occur. This is the first hurdle.

The second barrier to overcome in becoming empathically awake is to fully acknowledge that, within your own internal processing, the other person *is* you via the fact that you have an inner reflection that witnesses their arrival. And you yourself *are* the other person. We are not separate. We are essentially a combined twin of realization.

In the initial stages however, you may be subject to the phenomenon of not being able to clearly view what you can't see, feel what you can't touch, and listen to what you can't hear. And if that internal arrival is misunderstood, the dominant program will simply take over.

When somebody communicates with you, they transmit their intent, which may be composed of control. Within the structure of their communication, which travels upon language, they will convey to you as a child: I need you to learn this because I want you to understand who I am, for I am your teacher.

The adult is automatically in the role of educator. Every single person that we meet is our teacher when we are children. And as we are learning how to speak, the vibration within the sentence structure is very important. It impacts the feeling capacity of the young human being to decipher what is going on.

When you have somebody talking to you they may bring ten words, and within that sequence there is emotion attached to what they are conveying as information. As you get to maybe the fifth word, there's a sensation of guilt that lands in your being! It's a projection that is implanted within the sentence that you are learning as a feeling.

The person imparting this was incapable of understanding the process of how they themselves learnt to turn their feeling into emotion, which they then give to you in the structure of their sentence as a word to make you feel guilty.

You are burdened with this emotion and you say to yourself: "I feel guilty, but I don't know why." This is how you are coercively maneuvered by a casual interaction to do what you shouldn't do. And there you've lost a certain portion of your personal power.

What was there before that socializing influence was a pure interpretation system of feeling, which is meant to give you the capacity to put insight into a verbal context that contains information compacted within it, like a holographic image.

When words arise from your heart, or a feeling comes to you, you may see something visual, and if not there are many other ways to receive the vibration that contains the frequency of an insight you are destined to encounter. This process has got nothing to do with thinking. It has everything to do with your internal realization as the feeling arises.

Here you put your words to your insights, for you understand exactly what you see. You don't have to be told what you are receiving. You don't need somebody to interpret what your feeling is. You absorb it, and then you've got to find the words to communicate the realization.

The insight is a very, very important issue. It's wordlessly conveyed and pops up inside of you without any hindrance by an internal dialogue. It is completely free of that process. At that point of arrival it is still independent of the programming, but as it arises it gets interfered with by the script, for this is the modus operandi of social engineering.

This gradual schooling emanates from every corner of reality. It will initially impact you from your family environment and all the extended relations beyond that point who pack all these emotions in and start to solidify the age that you are going to mature to, in terms of your emotionality. This is the societal Trojan horse.

For example, if a significant portion of distorted feeling is established at the age of five, a human being may have difficulty growing beyond this emotional threshold as a consequence of its gravitational pull. This is not to underestimate the five-year-old awareness, which is highly advanced in terms of their ability to instantaneously assimilate and arrange a reality as it truly is in front of them. The brilliance of this young individual is rearranged by the social eddy, thus bypassing its natural creativity.

A child at this particular stage of development is extraordinarily aware in comparison to an adult who has been indoctrinated into the repetitive dogma of rote learning. Their high level of absorption is comparable to a supercomputer, organizing every facet of information without delay; and here we can realize the pure root of the empathic foundation that an adult human being would employ as their futuristic skill, were they not interrupted by the program.

At this point we have to ask ourselves: What stops us from accessing these intelligences? How do we become so caught up in the distortion?

Our natural empathic ability gets confused as a result of the emotional dogma besetting the infant's primary view, which would become the adult's capacity of absorption of the influx of information to be interpreted.

That unsettling import is transferred through resonant fields of density that establish an internal vibration by employing subtle shades of manipulation. Even if those transmissions are deemed socially acceptable, they are actually a normalized form of abuse that entrap awareness within the psyche of the person who is trying to convince you of what they believe *they* can't grow through, due to their own emotional immaturity.

Imagine that you are in a situation where you need to express your truth, and you start crying as though you are five years old, beset with a feeling of helplessness and despondency, knowing that you have been misunderstood.

Even though we truly know what is occurring, we are so occupied with the engineered consciousness that is bypassing our empathic view, which has never been allowed to mature into self-confident realization, that we can't cope with an exchange that challenges us to rise above the embedded entrapment.

What happens at this point of emotional immaturity? One fights for the wrong reasons, and within that confusion one has difficulty arriving home to the true insight that needs to be expressed. That raw realization is so deeply buried under the social emotion that it is virtually impossible to locate what can't be found; yet it is hiding in plain sight.

The child inside the adult's chest cries to be understood, though from the perspective of a socially engineered frame of reference the adult's empathic ability appears to be their immaturity. But this is not the case.

The engineered emotionality is smothering the truth, so the socially governed individual reverts back to their trained emphasis, *away* from the true feeling, to reflect upon their time of sorrow where they have been deeply misunderstood. The devastation of being misunderstood is all that's left of the empath's view.

This is how an empath's ability transmutes into the tears of remorse that are transferred into the social interaction, which bears emphasis towards the wrong issue, in essence forgetting the simple necessity of empathy and compassion. In other words, all that's left of the empath are tears, and the rage of the social program then takes over to reveal its dysfunction, which in reality is its true functionality.

When you look at it from this perspective, you can see that the emotion and the feeling are two very different things. We don't know how to interpret the feeling, and we don't know how to deal with the immaturity of the emotion that we are supposed to process, so we try to conceal our confusion and begin to apply the dysfunctional strategies that have been given to us as examples from our environment.

Our empathic nature is abused when we are young via the fact that we are an open vessel. We must all understand that if someone is prepared to guilt you they are actually readily drawing your feelings into an emotional context that renders you serviceable. They imprison you. And they know what they are doing.

The slight of hand takes place in plain sight. But nobody recognizes what is in full view because everybody is focused on the cognitive system, which in actuality is neuro-linguistically engineered.

We have two distinct systems of interpretation, and the

one that we are almost exclusively functioning with now is neuro-linguistics, which has been brought forward as a method to interpret human consciousness. It is essentially a set of cues detailing what people are going to do and where they're at; whether they are emotional or they are feeling, and if they are auditory or visually oriented. These are just the basics of that programming.

Over the last hundred years, a group of oligarchs engineered the information now applied to humanity at large for the purposes of domination, studiously implementing the principles of repetitive indoctrination to every generation in conjunction with emergent technologies.

Be aware that each new wave of youth has less real information and more unnecessary activities to be occupied within. One of these tactical inserts into the communal landscape is political correctness, which has resulted in an immense social pressure to stand in defense of that which is reasonably indefensible.

Using these strategies, autocratic forces are able to assert an inordinate influence upon one's personal narrative, ultimately steering the collective through a connective network of consciousness that can be redirected very easily via the fact that we are empathically attuned, as the hundredth monkey syndrome demonstrates.

Through repetition we are trained within that corrupt program. We are seen as a group that can be controlled because of this. The prejudices of social engineering are expressly designed to mute the possibility of our true situational consciousness manifesting.

Have we evolved to the point where we now understand that our consciousness can be manipulated via being subject to sound, whether we hear it or not?

Here I would like to suggest that you don't use LED light bulbs, for this will disturb the deeper visual functions of your eyes. These disruptive frequencies are also absorbed directly through the skin and recalibrate our biofield in a way that weakens immunity and mutes awareness. Do your research and you will discover this for yourself.

Our bodies are natural receivers of light, and our capacity to be in communion with the subtleties of what I am describing will be severely compromised if one is subject to damaging light sources on a continual basis. Even when you go to bed at night and there is artificial light coming from outside, filtering into your bedroom slightly, this will inhibit your body's ability to produce melatonin, which is a very important hormone that relates to the vital functions of your pineal gland.

If you can take into full consideration that we are vibration attuning itself to every circumstance, then it will be easy to comprehend the ramifications of focused frequencies upon our state of being as a biological organism.

Here I am only outlining the effects of everyday technologies that have been situationally placed in our personal environments, which have profoundly detrimental repercussions upon the natural cascade of the endocrine system and via this fact invariably alter one's consciousness.

For instance, frequencies emanating from Wi-Fi routers contribute enormously to our inability to be receptive to subtle vibratory fields. If you put seedlings too close to a router, even in full sunlight, only five percent will germinate but will not flourish. Their natural ability to thrive is severely compromised by that electromagnetic interference.

This crisis will only increase in severity when 5G is introduced, for the increased radiation being emitted invariably damages the very structure of our DNA. One very disturbing fact about 5G is that it travels upon frequencies that allow parasites and pathogens to proliferate uninterrupted, thereby gaining such momentum that they become impervious to allopathic and natural medicines.

These technological implementations are impacting our natural empathic abilities. Consider this and ask yourself why so many of us are not completely open. These are just some of the reasons. But do not despair. Becoming aware of this is enough to strengthen one's consciousness to go beyond it. Receiving this information will allow you to be openly defiant and less amenable to circumstances that are unnatural.

In other words, your consciousness will determine to

accept what can't be changed and change what is unacceptable. This will give you the ability to overcome all situational barriers coveting one's heart awareness, and thereby become fully receptive to true empathic attunement.

When an empath speaks, their words emerge from a knowing that hasn't been repetitively learnt. A lot of the time the reason these frequential insights can't be absorbed is that we have been subject to a massive campaign that has subverted our consciousness through the mechanisms of rote learning. This pre-formatting of perception, combined with disruptive technological influences, inhibit an individual from comprehending what is necessary to be assimilated in the living moment.

A feeling arising is immediately known as internal wisdom to be spoken by an empath, yet may escape an individual caught within the process of trying to internalize that information through the syndrome of a repetitious dialogue that in essence blocks what it cannot understand, thus reverting back to dogma and missing everything that was said.

The reason this cognitive lapse occurs is that the empathic

communication doesn't carry identifiable points of reference embedded in the words. The one in reception misses the content portrayed through emptiness via the fact that nothing is attached to this import of information other than that formless internal wisdom produced by the frequency of the heart to be spoken.

This is how the trained emotional response gets in the way and blocks a person from actually hearing something that may assist them in their evolution. When communication doesn't contain the vibration that they've been programmed to react to, it bypasses them. They miss it completely!

It is difficult to reiterate upon a point of wisdom, for once you start to repeat yourself, the insight becomes a dogma. Wisdom has to be stated, with feeling, a different way every time. When someone simply repeats what they have read or heard elsewhere it may sound beautiful, until you discover that the person behind the words has not embodied what they have spoken.

If the need arises to relay something more than once, an empath will always find new ways to articulate that relate directly to the vibratory essence of that particular circumstance. This is the momentary nature of an empathic reality. The seer will receive volumes of information via light fibers that conduct pure content through the inaudible frequency that has been seen.

How this occurs is that in the physiology of the eyes there are cones, not unlike whirlpools, which interpret information in spiraling vortices that travel into the hippocampus and at that point are reverse engineered via a zero-point that is unknown to itself, which will appear as words emanating from the heart.

This is where you simultaneously travel into your own reservoirs of wisdom, by ninety-eight percent observing your own empty reflection while the one you are interacting with gives you a window into their world of suffering.

Experience is transmuted into compassionate empathy that has nothing to do with what happened to you, but everything to do with the other person's dilemma.

If everybody becomes aware of this never-ending state of flux, then the ebbs and flows of creativity will bring definition to the characteristics of what you are realizing at every single moment. Language is currently our primary mode of communication, but this is not the way it used to be done. We related with feeling first and language second.

The transferal and acquisition of words into the mind was less important than the emphasis of realization, which contains the encoded information that is transported upon a frequential bandwidth of mutual understanding.

Through listening to what can't be heard, by seeing what is invisible, by knowing that which cannot be known, an empath emerges. The light has truly been misinterpreted via semantics. Language has many points of reference that distort this luminous import into corroborative points, which becomes the truth of real misunderstanding.

As a wise man once said, "In the beginning there was the word." Yet it never existed, thus disappearing from view, and was at no point contained within the mind, nor had it need to explain itself.

The Ghost

When we observe the pure content of our gestures, we are witnessing the essence of who we really are.

Who are you?

Who am I?

I'm a physical body that is symbiotically connected to feeling. I'm a human being contained within a physical form, which is all designed to uphold this reality.

The physiological arrangement that houses our essence is profoundly aware of everything that occurs. The reason the perceptual facility of the body is so difficult to understand is that it is an automated process that works in exactly the same way as our lungs or heart or any other internal organ does. It functions and is aware on our behalf.

The body consciousness that abides within this temple is a gesture of service for the being that is momentarily traveling within this dimensional reality. And this being is you.

A few important questions must be asked:

What do I put into this physical body?

What do I breathe?

What do I drink?

What do I eat?

We've looked extensively at the emotional program, and now we need to examine the automated internal system that contains us as a transdimensional being within a physical realm for a brief period of time, housing the eyes, ears and heart process which becomes the words that we must travel upon.

Through our reflective observance, we eventually realize that we have a faculty, a river of chi, that carries light photons into our bio-electromagnetic field. It is our breath.

Upon birth we inhale this vital force in, and upon the point of death we exhale that potential out. It contains all the processes of remembrance, and gives rise to everything imaginable in terms of our capacity as a perceiver to create within the world that we have entered into.

The breath is a very subtle key. It is the gateway for our eyes and our ears to listen and witness. It is such a non-obtrusive part of our perception that we can easily overlook it, unless we are directed to realize that this river of alchemy is one of the ultimate perceivers that leads us to see the path which we must walk upon as gently as we possibly can.

The breath is extremely akin to water, like twins born from the womb of life, they are unwaveringly connected to each other and to the silent mind.

The intention of the breath can be watched carefully, and can be listened to intensely, especially when it is an inaudible process. Our empty commander, our pure void substance, our mind, witnesses intangibly the breath, via the fact that it is actually not there, if you don't talk to yourself.

It is only upon the intervention of thought that all these magical elements can be lost, through the confusing malaise of the internal dialogue. If we learn to observe our breath, profound things can occur.

This delicate equilibrium can be jeopardized if a person's physiology is disrupted by consuming the wrong foods and being subject to disruptive feelings from their environment. An empath can't function in clouds of anger or animosity.

Empaths need to be housed in supportive environments where an atmosphere of openness prevails, and feel a sense of acceptance in order to attune to this very acute and delicate vibration that is called communication. This is a complex thing to come to terms with, as we require a sustainable community to actually bring children up as intuitive beings that mature into finely tuned empaths.

Food programming is another enormous subject to take into consideration, for it sets up the process of hidden emotional expectations, which become covert desires and will work in conjunction with the internal dialogue.

The feeling of wanting something external to oneself turns into an emotional addiction, which takes you away from your own essential nature and the feelings that need to be focused upon in order for one to be empathically attuned.[iii] This reflects the same principle of *presents* versus *presence*, as outlined in *Whisperings of the Dragon.*

When a person is fed the wrong foods, the whole organism falls into a low resonance state that inhibits the higher functioning potential of the human entity. Polluting the body is a very direct way to take an empath off their path, for ill health distorts perception and brings a person into a reality of separation.

[iii] Reclaiming your eating program is one of the most empowering means to instigate deep transformation within your life. If you are interested in changing your habits in terms of your food addictions, please go to **www.rawfoodsolution.com** and contact my wife, Mizpah Matus, for a wealth of information and personalized support on your journey to vibrant health.

In the so-called *normal world,* there is a tacit understanding that says, "I'm not going to be open and I'm not going to help you, since no one is going to support or care for me."

In an empath's world, we say: "I'm open. Enter my field of energy so I can interpret your feelings and speak the truth of what needs to be done. I'm here for you."

But this is not happening, and we have become acclimatized to that underlying sense of danger, which is a trap; yet another barrier to prevent the empathic view from coming forward. Once everybody realizes these factors we can begin to decipher the complexity of what we are faced with.

Now we understand that we've got our feelings and our body consciousness, which attempts to instigate change by making us aware of deranged emotions appearing within the physiology.

The next covert factor to contend with is the relentless internal dialogue. This is the key element of destructive manipulation within the Trojan horse mentality of installing cloaked elements within that are meant to infiltrate your sovereign state of being; a false proposition that can't be interfered with via the fact that you think it is meant to be there.

You look at this and you ask: How did the Trojan horse begin? Why do we talk to ourselves inside of our minds? The reason we do this is that we can't cope with the emotions we harbor within, which have been purposefully cultivated through a complex layering of social engineering.

Feelings originate from the heart, and instead of rising up through the throat and manifesting as elegant communication that is received in kind, these impulses for true expression are circumvented into an uncomfortable feeling inside your organs, primarily your liver.

This governing organ, one of our main distributors of blood and chi in the body, becomes congested by the accumulation of toxins that are stored in the fats. Unable to initiate the natural transformational process of metabolism and regulation of the correct dispersion of vital fluids and energy within the human organism, the overloaded liver affects the physiology by sending repetitive signals of discomfort, which indicates that a form of stagnancy has begun to influence the consciousness of the host.

Traveling upon the liver meridian and up into the silent command center, these dysfunctional directives emulate the flow of empathic communication (which is in actuality authentic quantum entanglement) in a parallel process of limited engagement that is entirely scripted; forged upon disruptive emotions and baseless assumptions endlessly echoing within the mechanisms of the mind; thus circumventing the heart.

This unnatural state of being, vibrating with its own adaptive intelligence, successfully propagates the activation of the social program. It is an installed, automated process within the physiology, which makes it very hard for the individual to recognize what is occurring without identifying with that dilemma as their own personal dysfunction.

Although it looks like nothing is being done to us, the intricacies of this enculturation process were set in motion long ago, and it has since gathered enormous momentum.

Religious and cultural insertions originating from the ancient Sumerians were installed thousands of years ago to secure the imprisonment of our mind, effectively begetting biological enslavement through the manipulation of the psyche. These original frequential adjustments are now becoming meticulously attuned through the technologies we are arriving upon.

This multilayered, psychobiological inheritance is a form of entanglement that doesn't have to be re-engineered, for it self-replicates, generation after generation, in a numbing self-similar fashion that adapts in comparison to the time one is born in. So that you can understand how this complex bane on humanity thrives and remains largely undetected, imagine it from this perspective.

Everybody has different sized bones, different shaped bodies. The bone structure of one's face is always distinct to somebody else's. Even in the same family, each person's features are individualized. Every human being has its own signature in terms of the emanating force of the vibration created via the vessel that one resides within.

Therefore, when one person gets angry next to another person, we can easily overlook the similarity, and that is why we are not noticing that what is happening is a repetitive eddy. The variance absorbs our capacity to realize that we are being subject to the same things over and over again in slightly modified guises.

Every individual's internal functionality exhibits the different strengths and weaknesses that are inherent within their genome. Each organ vibrates with its own independent frequency within a symbiotic process, and although they work in harmony they are actually under grave duress from the general toxicity and stress that we are subject to these days.

Our internal arrangement can be seen as a form of sacred geometry that has been warped by accommodating an unwholesome lifestyle. Once you gain this overview, it is easy to conceive of how this very delicate balance can be interfered with.

The manipulation of our physical frequencies is a pure science that has been purposefully withheld for reasons of control. The human body houses over 2,600 distinct vibrational codes that can be detected, isolated and altered with a degree of subtlety that is unfathomable to the general populace.

It is very easy to disrupt a human being by normalizing a dysfunctional dietary status quo through repetitive advertising that assures everybody that what they are eating is safe and wholesome. I will illustrate a simple example of this before I expand upon how the mind becomes infiltrated by the liver.

We will only cover one point here, but it is a very relevant issue within society: human beings consuming milk after they have finished suckling on the nutrients provided by a mother's breast.

Beyond the point of being weaned, one need never include milk in their diet again. This is a controversial subject, but the crux of the matter is that dairy eventually blocks the lymphatic system, setting off a cascade of maladies.

It is widely promoted over the whole planet that if women want to have strong bones they should drink milk. In the early 1960's there was even a policy instituted to supply various types of flavored milk to children at school, under the devious premise that this will provide protein and strengthen the skeletal system.

In actuality, being subject to over-consumption of dairy (all milk products) one's system becomes slowly clogged, and upon this gradually ensuing consequence - alongside the advent of increasing environmental toxins and coupled with other ill-advised dietary choices - the body becomes incapable of dealing with the natural process of detoxification.

As a result, the lymphatic system becomes so severely stagnated that the kidneys and all filtering systems of the body begin to shut down. And remember, at the moment I am only talking about milk products. Though dairy has been strongly affirmed to be the main supplement that one needs to fortify bones, unfortunately this is not the truth.

In essence, what milk consumption does is cause acidosis within the physical disposition, not only surrounding the organs but also within the joints. This acid-forming syndrome within the body is then remedied by our own internal physiology by drawing upon the calcium of our skeletal system to help the body eliminate the acidosis. In other words, dairy weakens your bones.

This is only one example, as I have said, and it is directly related to the sweeping lies being perpetuated in terms of the masses being convinced through institutionalized brainwashing that proven biohazards such as milk products are a safe and even necessary dietary requirement.

Now, you may be saying to yourself at this moment, "I drink milk, and I feel healthy and strong." There are some people that can get away with it and many of us that cannot. It depends on one's physical disposition in terms of one's genetics being able to cope with diverse situations.

If you are at this point listening to me very carefully, you will begin to understand that it is what you are consuming that allows you to be consumed, through being misled and by not understanding that you have the power to change your destiny by feeding your body with the most essential elements it needs, which originate from a raw and cooked vegan perspective.

Over the last four generations, worldwide, the human genome has been compromised extensively, and what we are failing to realize is that illness begins to appear as dysfunctional emotions first. For example, anger, jealousy, impatience, cruelty, possessiveness, not wanting to share, or willfully going out of one's way to hurt another human being. These are all the beginning of sickness, the first signs of its arrival. Even the inability to understand what somebody else is going through is a malformation of the original view, which is naturally empathic.

Everybody *understands* what they are meant to do but nobody *knows* what to do, for the decision-making capacity of an emotionally stagnant awareness doesn't have the fluidity to move beyond its current illusion.

How can you find your personal power if you are blocked in emotion instead of traveling upon the pure feeling that you are meant to interpret? And how can you have insights if your mind gets in the way?

Let's get back to the liver and take a look at how this warrior commander can be misled to become the enemy of the state, and then direct its treachery towards the sovereign kingdom, which is one's heart.

In certain ancient wisdom traditions, a human being who had no substance was looked upon as a ghost. The unfortunate reality of being haunted has an extremely close relationship to what is happening to humankind at this moment in time. The temple we abide within is being occupied, or possessed.

Whether one is simple-minded or exaggerated within the extremes of a manipulative intelligence, every degree within this spectrum of awareness can be influenced via an internal coup that arises from liver imbalance. Dumb is dangerous, and smart is even more dangerous than dumb, when not under the command of the heart.

To examine this haunting phenomenon, we will look at the maladies surrounding a dysfunctional liver from an Oriental perspective, and briefly touch upon healing and the art of war, simultaneously. These fields are very similar in terms of their application to life, whether as an external manifestation or an inner state of being that reveals one's internal energetics.

The most sacred position, where the heart abides within our temple, is centered directly within our sternum, and is known as the heart chakra. This is the hub of our toroidal field, governing both physical and energetic integrity. In every human being the strengths and fallibilities of one's genetic heritage will influence what manifests as a result of incorrect lifestyle choices.

We must also take into account the environmental toxins that surround us, which are adversely affecting our immune system and manipulating the health of our genome.

Like frogs in hot water, we are not noticing what is creeping up on us. Scientific studies have shown that frogs will happily sit in water that is being gradually heated to boiling point and not know they are being cooked until it is too late. This is what is occurring environmentally to us as human beings. We are progressively becoming more afflicted and cannot adapt to what is happening to us, via a denial that is connected to liver dysfunction.

This overwhelming dilemma causes a type of atrophy that affects intelligence, and disallows the masses from realizing that we are becoming severely genetically impaired as a result of toxic exposure. What is occurring is a form of biological warfare, which includes geo-engineering programs that have been operational since 1985.

Our environment and our food are being weaponized. The higher the accumulation of heavy metals and pollutants, the more physically and mentally deranged we all become. This profoundly alters our consciousness from being fully functional within the heart to becoming subordinate to the domineering malaise of the liver.

In Oriental philosophy[iv], the metaphor of the heart is a representation of a king ruling over his subjects with kindness and compassion, whereas the liver's station is the king's general who protects the royal family and the populace from invading marauders, silently moving through the lands as an undetectable guardian.

Seen from this Oriental medical perspective, if the general becomes imbalanced it will attempt to dethrone the king and steal

---

[iv] During the Chinese Cultural Revolution, one very important medical text on the internal alchemy of the heart was withdrawn from circulation, for this vital esoteric information gave people the power of independence in terms of fortifying their sovereign ability to decide what is right or wrong within their own lives.

the freedom and the wealth of the populace behind the royal family's back, undermining all equilibrium that has been established. Thus the liver becomes an indoor enemy, a shadow of who it is meant to be, and this is what is known as the *Hun,* which means *ghost* in Mandarin.

We have to unravel this internal mutiny, which has been manufactured by our external environment to affect us in a way that creates this Trojan horse situation. How this occurs inside the physical body is that the organs can only withstand a certain amount of toxins within the system, and when there is an overload the liver becomes agitated.

From that point onwards, it operates as a strange protagonist that steals from every other organ possible it's feelings and resources, including the sovereign command of our heart; not too dissimilar to the story of the moneylenders mentioned in the chapter called, *The Receptive Heart.*

In Chinese medicine there is a meridian[v] for every organ, but there is no meridian for the brain. This is an indication that the mind is meant to be clear, void of thought. This silent command center views its own emptiness, and in so doing allows the heart to rise and be spoken through the throat chakra, invariably enabling the ears to hear what has never been heard before, and the eyes to see what unveils itself to be known. This is the pathway of the heart that reveals our true status as human beings.

When the liver is no longer in harmony it becomes the possessive Hun, the ghost that rises up through the liver meridian and takes over. The pathway of the liver meridian runs up through the throat, influencing pure communication, then opens to the eyes, affecting sight in terms of inhibiting true seeing, and ends at the crown of the head, which adversely impacts our empty command center - our connective link to the universe at large –

[v] A meridian is an electromagnetic pathway that runs through the body. There are twelve main meridians that are each connected to the various organs.

almost invariably in cooperation with an internal dialogue, which completes the whole disruption.

Another branch of the liver meridian circles the mouth, distorting speech through internal discomfort that becomes a grimace of anger. These are all expressions of frequential dysfunction, which causes a system imbalance. When the Hun is in command of this vital pathway, it becomes a metaphorical noose that cuts off the ascension process of the heart.

When the liver is working in harmony there is an absolute free and easy feeling, an abandon, a joyful happiness that accompanies us within every action. Under these conditions we don't feel its presence at all. It is our silent support system. However, when the liver becomes deranged and agitated, the gallbladder[vi], working in cahoots with its disharmony, rises violently and can be felt in the temples, disrupting the eyes and distorting our view of the world.

[vi] The gallbladder is paired with the liver in Traditional Chinese Medicine.

What is important to realize is that when the liver takes this position of defiance it transforms into the Hun, the foreign installment; that deranged spirit that travels upon the electrical pathway of the liver meridian through its internal agitation, toward and into the brain to reveal itself as the false prophet: The internal dialogue.

This imposter will speak to the affected individual and discuss and bargain with what has been heard and delivered from the heart, directly to the ears. The internal dialogue will bring into question what the eyes see, and upon this point will commandeer the throat and mouth to speak on its behalf, thereby bypassing the heart's direct expression of truth.

This is the true foreign installment. There are many ways to induce and sustain this phenomenon, and these undermining strategies are well known by the elite's of old and new.

Endless stories have been injected into humanity about a beast possessing us, but in reality this diabolical cultural insertion is just part of a Luciferian agenda propagated by our own species to control the masses. The grossly distorted biases we are subject to have been even more smoothly assimilated in recent times via our relationship with relentlessly occupying technology.

Every resource has been mobilized in this hidden war against the growth of human consciousness towards its collective empowerment. No expense has been spared to keep us from remembering who we really are: Sovereign, intuitive empaths.

THE MANTRA OF LIFE

Let us now examine *dharma, adharma,* and *the abyss.* I mentioned in a previous chapter that we would have a close look at the techniques of *mantras* and *sutras,* but I am not going to approach this in a traditional way.

We will travel to the origin of these principle arts, and discover how they have been watered down to represent elements that, in a practical sense, are not really functional. I would like you to imagine that you are accompanying me, experiencing these philosophies within an alternate timeline. In essence, recovering a lost heritage is our primary aim here.

We will first consider the concept of *mantra* within the context of *adharma,* and then proceed to the positive elements to establish an alternate view that may surprise you. You will see how these elegantly complex practices were originally empathically oriented, attuned to the silent ebbs and flows of a constant vigil of silence, which is the abyss.

Adharma is the concept of concentrating on that which is opposed to a path with heart. It is the art of willful intent that wishes to obtain power through nefarious means. In other words: the black hat.

Dharma is the pursuit of transparent honesty through upholding a righteous view to act with purpose for the betterment of all. This is the white hat.

The abyss, which represents emptiness, may be the more elusive of the three to grasp. To be in devotion towards your circumstances is to apply the art of neutrality, neither being *good,* nor *bad* but in essence to act appropriately with a kind heart, never looking for recognition, never expecting returns through design.

From the perspective of adharma, a person will act selfishly, only concerned with the outcome for themselves. They do not care about the consequences of their actions upon another or the suffering they may cause.

Not too dissimilar to a ruthless businessman who creates jobs and feeds the mouths of many, yet pollutes a river or a stream, which may cause devastation to an entire region and have future ramifications that negate the positivity of employment by rendering the environment unproductive for a generation.

As you can see from this example, the black hat can generate some positive results, such as bringing prosperity, but the overall return on their actions is detrimental, and the driving intent is unscrupulously mercenary.

Dharma, the white hat, may be religiously inclined, righteous, bearing goodwill and wishing to benefit all. However, as we know, doing good things under the banner of self-righteousness can hide a twisted character, or may propel a kind-hearted person to make bad decisions that harm the community in the long run.

Under the guise of religion, much suffering has been inflicted over the ages. Religious dogma, even though it seems to be based upon spiritual ideals and higher principles, provides a simple, well-intentioned man with bias and limitations that may harm another. For example, he may restrict his wife from certain activities, which inevitably are her right of expression: to evolve in pursuits that bring her enjoyment and freedom.

Both adharma and dharma can be religiously inclined, and each has the potential to bring harm and restriction through bias. We are currently steadily moving through the difficult phase of understanding that religions - whether noble or diabolical, orthodox or liberal - have deeply embedded within them the seeds of cognitive dissonance via the relentless integration of agenda into their application, individually and collectively; and equally through misrepresentation of that which has not really been understood.

Moving beyond these polarities, we arrive upon the art of emptiness, neutrality, or the abyss. Here we have the most difficult art to master: To act in accordance with each circumstance appropriately, attempting at every moment not to cause harm, nor to turn the eyes of an innocent individual toward darkness and retribution; never to lead any circumstance towards self-righteousness, which appears as a rigidity that does not yield its softness to the moment, to be discovered within the service of that perception.

This is the art of the empath. To be there yet not to be there simultaneously, forever watching the rising and falling of good and bad, sadness and happiness, positive and negative. To be subject to what cannot be known, attentively listening to what cannot be heard; to wait patiently to view what cannot be seen; to feel with abandon what cannot be touched and to joyously witness that which is unknowable.

An empath introspectively reflects the awareness of adharma and dharma as a play that appears on the stage of life to be eternally observed, bearing constant witness to these two elements that bring about the reality that life is suffering. Each endures the other, in an endless dance of illusions.

The seer will receive every circumstance, every human being within every encounter, as an opportunity to learn about themselves. To see the rising and falling of their feelings as they communicate with the frequencies which are the inaudible sounds emanating from each circumstance to be felt. Their journey is an endless river that is sometimes calm and cool, other times tumultuous and rough, as they watch the world from a vantage point that is as delicate as a transparent bubble that can be perforated by a mere glance.

Many techniques have been employed through the history of humanity to obtain enlightenment, and one of the tools utilized in diverse cultures around the world is the *mala*. These are beads that are strung upon a string. The number of beads will differ, depending on where they originate, but for this example let's say we have a mala with 108 beads. A mala is used for meditation, and within most meditative practices a mantra is given as a means to focus awareness.

As a yogi pulls one bead over the index finger, the string in between the beads will rest upon this digit. And as he pulls the next bead across, he repeats the mantra within his mind, which is counted by the bead. This is so that the yogi does not have to enumerate and recite simultaneously a mantra. He knows that at the end of the mala there will be a tassel, and this marker represents the completion of one cycle: 108 repetitions of that mantra.

There is a secret hidden here, but I won't disclose it yet, about the bead itself. Remind me later to tell you, and as you read, realize I am laughing to myself and smiling, knowing that I will fulfill this promise, which is your question. You are in my future and I am in your past. Or are you in my past and I in your future? Time is interesting. Does it even really exist? Nevertheless, let's move on.

The string in between the beads represents *samadhi*: joyfully being contained within one's silence, the abyss, a time of emptiness until the next repetition occurs, which is the next mantra to appear.

This method is meant to train the mind to focus upon a command, which at this point is the recitation, and when this transforms into a *sutra* - which is a representation of an act of power, the wishing for a result – this then manifests the next containment, which is called a *siddhi.*

A siddhi is when one obtains a special power that comes about in relation to the command given. Many yogic practitioners look for this result as an indication of progression on their path of development. But remember, though these techniques have been universally employed throughout the world at different times, they can become stumbling blocks upon one's path if misunderstood.

What I am to reveal to you now is an abstract story that contains the exact same truths and techniques I have just mentioned. The string of the mala represents a time of waiting: emptiness.

What if I were to tell you I am this emptiness? I am this abyss. I am samadhi, the intuitive empath, and I would like to convey to you how to respond to the world around you as if you were a mala: 108 beads upon a string that represents the pre-determined destiny of your life.

Your time of waiting, your time of service, your observance of the moments which are continually escaping you; in essence, your path with heart. I am your teacher, and you are my student, wishing to understand how to proceed.

When *adharma* approaches me, I am the string that is wrapped over the index finger, determining the weight. The technique I use is to grab the next bead with my thumb, to roll it over my digit and proceed forwards with silence and abandon; to feel the impact of adharma approaching and act accordingly with that person, neither submitting, nor rejecting.

Not influencing but just observing, watching the feelings moving through my chest, my whole being affected by this experience. Adharma becomes my mala bead; my living mantra that speaks to me. Not inside my head as a word but outside of me as a mantra, whispering to me which way to proceed.

I watch gently this mantra attempting to become a sutra, as a force that wishes to influence and direct my being toward an outcome. The sun sets, the moon arises, I sleep within the silence, a dreamless slumber.

The morning appears. The weight of the string of my 108th mala bead calls me to retrieve the next jewel, my mantra. On this day I meet *dharma*, the white hat. Dharma now becomes my mantra. I act in service and kindness towards this being, in exactly the same fashion that I responded to adharma. Yet today, dharma is my mantra.

Dharma looks at me knowingly, trying to influence my path, attempting to change the mantra into a sutra of influence. The sun sets. The moon arises. The freshness of the morning appears.

Upon my index finger lays the string of my mala: my silence, my samadhi, the happiness that exists in between the people I meet; the emptiness, the absorption that shines from my eyes as I communicate to each mantra that attempts to turn my quietude into a command. But I cannot be directed. It seems that I defiantly stand in resistance of that which wishes to obtain my favor. I disappear from it. I was never there.

Every person that we meet on our path is the bead of our mala, is the mantra that wishes to obtain the suggestion, the power of a sutra, which is the result. I haven't yet explained exactly what a mantra or a sutra is and how they work. Traditionally, a mantra is a phrase or a word with a particular vibration (often in

Sanskrit) utilized to interrupt the mind, to stop it from thinking and to focus those internal thoughts to become the recitation itself.

For example, a mantra can be as simple as, "I am". When the mind goes to this, the internal dialogue is meant to stop. But the contradiction is that the dialogue is replaced by a repeated phrase, mimicking what is already there. We have to remember that the primary objective here is to reach silence in between each mantra.

A sutra is the ability to command a word within the mind to manifest as a tangible outcome. For example: *The strength of an elephant* is a sutra. If a man were to obtain the power of this beast, he would be unstoppable. And when the sutra manifests within the body of the man, it is called a siddhi, the end result. Should we seek these mystical powers? I would say not.

As an intuitive empath I would relay to you in quiet humbleness that the next person I meet is my mantra. I have no need for the mantra to become a sutra. I wish to control nothing. And thus I wish not to be controlled.

Yet only kindness and compassion are awaiting for my next mantra to appear in front of me. The words and the intentions are expressed on the outside, not the inside. The verbal content appears in the heart as feeling to be spoken immediately, never arising to the mind.

In other words, you can't think it, you can only know it. And if you know it you would never bother to think it. The mind is not meant to be concentrated in this way. It is to be empty of itself, filled with the abyss, with neutrality. Mindful observance has no contours, it is without shape or definition. This is the responsibility that resides within the domain of the heart: to forget itself whilst being fully engaged within its task.

The silent commander just looks at what it cannot see, and listens to what it cannot hear by virtue of the fact that it's not talking to itself. One's eyes become a strange intermediary that realizes that the heart is sending visual signals on invisible pathways that become the words that are to be spoken.

Once this arrival recedes quietly into the background, one's internal perception will then wait patiently for the next event to occur as that elusive content arising from within. When you experience this you will begin to understand your own personal transmissions.

The ears wait patiently, for they know that nothing will be spoken until a feeling appears. And if you happen to be sitting quietly by yourself then watch this arrival and with your silent breath this will become your meditation, your vehicle of discovery, your personal path with heart.

My destiny, my path, my mantra, appears in front of me at every moment, and I am contained within those gestures, and of service to them. For you are the string. You are the mala. You are my destiny. My heart will speak to you and what I have to say will never enter my mind to be formulated before the words are spoken. This is the divine decree of an empath, an intuitive seer.

Now that these particular principles have been defined, we can observe two types of meditation. One is empathic, and the other can be misleading. Only one point off north. That is all that is needed. Decide for yourself the truth. Practice the techniques and see what you obtain. One will beckon results. The other will want for nothing, in peace proceeding forward.

Know that the abstract tale and the acquisition of mantras, sutras and strings, are a representation of a mala: the next step you take in life. What if someone came along and turned this abstract tale into a concrete practice? Have you been misled?

For those of you who are being introduced to these concepts for the first time, the power of your life can now be discovered in the true practice of service, within these timeless principles that you may apply.

The Appearance of the Disappearing

The appearance of the disappearing is a subject of great subtlety and complexity. By way of entering into it, I would like to relay the story of some experiments that were conducted with simple containers of rice and water by a Japanese scientist called, Masuro Emoto, to share my own personal conclusions about this research and illustrate valuable information about our empathic journey on this planet.

Mr. Emoto filled three glass containers full of rice, covering the grains with water, just a few inches higher. All were filled to the same level and sealed. To the first container, he said, every day, "Thank you." To the second, he said, "You are a fool," and the third, he ignored completely.

At the end of one month, he opened up the first container and found that it was gently fermenting, with a surprisingly sweet aroma. The second one had turned black with mold. The third container was like a wretched swamp and stank of death.

I can confirm that all the experiments he conducted on water are true and verifiable, and you can corroborate this by looking into his research yourself. We will come back and reference this study as a vehicle of discovery to view very deeply the contradictions within human behavior.

The three containers provide a parallel subject to illuminate Dharma, Adharma and the Abyss, engaging our empathic capacity to occupy many positions simultaneously. This is our innate ability to understand from multiple perspectives via the mind's eye, and further, to access communication with beings that are transdimensionally active in terms of traversing these fields of perception. When one is clear about their empathic link, these apparently forgotten abilities become available.

Water is a universal medium that reflects this fluency. It exemplifies how we are meant to communicate on the frequency of feeling and helps us to understand that we need to learn to decipher the language embedded within the continuous vibrational exchange that we are subject to.

We ourselves are composed of between fifty-five to seventy-five percent water, depending on our age, and babies can be up to eighty percent water. Via the fact that when individuals are tested the water content varies slightly every time these percentages can change – in other words there are no absolutes – but on average the following water ratios can be observed in the organs and physiology, with the blood containing 83%, heart 73%, brain 75%, lungs 83%, muscles 78%, kidneys 83%, liver 86%, connective tissue 60%, skin 70%, bones 28% and fat 20%.

Let's take a moment to look at the phenomenon of food programming in relation to the water contained within fat. When a person eats processed and fast foods - that is, food devoid of natural photonic energy - that human being becomes toxically infused with this devitalized and contaminated material that carries incorrect frequencies for the body.

This gets stored as fat, as if it is a poison, and is transferred to the lymphatic system for elimination, thus overloading our physiology and eventually shutting down the kidney's ability to detoxify our living organism. Fat then acts as a barrier, inhibiting absorption of essential information that is contained within those subtle frequencies that recalibrate water to be empathically attuned to its environment.

This outer layer becomes an extremely efficient armor which blocks you from your own spiritual growth, and from understanding on a frequential level what is truly meant to be absorbed from your circumstances. Your sovereign right as a light being to evolve appropriately on your path is inextricably linked to this vital receptivity.

Studies also show that in overweight and obese individuals, especially past midlife, brain function will reveal a ten-year increase in age. In other words, surplus fat causes a significant deterioration of cerebral white matter, reflecting the effective age of a sixty year old, when your chronological age may be only fifty years old. This is why I always ask my students to eat raw, living food and attempt to detoxify the lymphatic system via losing the excess fat on their body.

Since we are comprised of such high water content, which is symbiotically mixing with every component that is contained within our human organism, we possess a very powerful cooperative network of intelligence that relies upon this liquid crystal for its optimum functioning.

Every fluid element in the body is supported by water, which is integral to the operation of the human physiology. If we take into consideration that each organ has a feeling, which emanates a frequency, then we can begin to understand that there is a mysterious reception occurring in terms of a silent communication taking place between all beings that we may encounter on our journey.

In parallel to the fact that the studies have confirmed that intention and thought forms can affect water, there is something even more profound occurring that we are all not noticing.

Scientists have acknowledged that they don't understand the living transformative properties of water, though they recognize that it is a fluid crystal that contains information.

It can be liquid, gaseous, or solid, and no other element on the planet can replicate its mutability. Another unusual trait of water is that it collects information and can also be de-programmed in many different ways. When it transforms from ice to liquid it loses its memory of previous experiences. The same renewal occurs when it coalesces from a cloud into raindrops.

This crucial transformational stage has been heavily interfered with by geo-engineering, and in particular through extensive chemtrailing all over our planet. Originating from the military-industrial complex and controlled by a ruthless oligarchy, our environment has been weaponized as part of an agenda of depopulation, with the eventual aim to gain greater control over a smaller amount of people within a one-world order.

With chemtrails a fine mist is carefully disseminated over the environment from planes specifically built for this function, which release their toxic payload into the upper stratosphere.

These pathogenic deposits contaminate the burgeoning cloud formations so that when the moisture coalesces it falls as pre-programmed droplets laden with pollutants, instead of undergoing the renewal process described above.

This rain has no vitality, nor enough emptiness to freely adapt to the new environment that it falls upon. Only the chemical information embedded is carried, which makes the water unfit for every single living organism, turning fertile soil excessively alkaline and destroying the natural diversity of our environment.

To give you an idea of the scope of what is occurring by virtue of the murderous intention directed towards us as a humanity, here is a list of the compounds that are spread knowingly over us:

Aluminum oxide particles, arsenic, bacilli and molds, barium salts, barium titanates, cadmium, calcium, chromium, desiccated human red blood cells, ethylene dibromid, enterobacter cloacae, enterobacteriaceae, human white blood cells - A (restrictor enzyme used in research labs to snip and combine DNA), lead, mercury, methyl aluminum, mold spores, morgellons, mycoplasma, nano-aluminum-coated fiberglass, nitrogen trifluoride, (known as CHAFF), nickel, polymer fibers, pseudomonas aeruginosa, pseudomonas florescens, radioactive cesium, radioactive thorium, selenium, serratia marcscens, sharp titanium shards, silver, streptomyces, stronthium, sub-micron particles (containing live biological matter), unidentified bacteria, uranium, and yellow fungal mycotoxins.[vii]

In undeveloped countries (which in actual fact is a misnomer) where black magic is active, it is well known that if a magician – a practitioner of Luciferian arts – would like to decrease the intelligence of their victim, they would place the blood of a dead man over the entrance of the front door of that person's home. The cellular information within this blood will then command their bodily fluids to return to the earth, in preparation for death.

[vii] Source: stopsprayingcalifornia.com

This technique is used to diminish one's spiritual capacity to ascend and evolve beyond one's current evolutionary phase, and this nefarious act will render the victim more pliable in terms of suggestion. In combination with these deadly metals and chemicals, the inclusion of human blood cells into the mix furthers the agenda of unconscionable interference with our natural environment and the internal energetics of humanity at large.

This is the disappearing of the appearing. What appears is what is not supposed to be there, and consequently we disappear from our personal path.

Now let's leave this terrible detour and return to the all-encompassing subject of water and how it is affected via its tumultuous journey through the circumstances it is confronted with in the 21st century.

This liquid crystal undergoes a dramatic reset process and loses its vitality through exposure to pollution or toxic environments, such as when moving through the network of pipes in a city. Here water obtains all the negative emotions of its inhabitants, as well as human feces and devastating chemicals such as chlorine and pharmaceutical toxins, just to name a few. The water collects this overload of pestilent residue and thereby loses the integrity of its crystalline structure.

This water, loaded with so much debris, is then consumed once again, delivering the environment's dysfunction back to its origin as information that integrates on a cellular level in the human physiology. As a result of this noxious cycle the water is deprived of the possibility to deprogram itself and start again as a cleansed entity, as are we.

This process that is being endlessly repeated at the moment should be great cause for concern and alarm. Has this been deliberately engineered to provoke a crisis in humanity that will lead us to decide to do the wrong things with our destiny? This is a question you have got to ask yourself.

Is this part of the disappearing of the appearing? Vanishing from yourself and becoming someone else who is unrecognizable. Are we being provoked to be in the wrong place at the wrong time, without understanding how this is occurring?

When you are aware of water and how its properties support us, you can completely comprehend the extent to which this ubiquitous element can be interfered with as a tactic to create a planetary crisis, where we find ourselves unknown to our true abilities.

In combination with the contaminated water we are consuming, the fear of war and conflict compounds a profound worldview of negativity and despair, which is a very low frequency state. Are we not then easier to control?

Most human beings can only handle one crisis at a time. We are being incrementally dosed with dozens of micro-crises, unaware of the implications of what is truly being done to us. Pollution is one very effective method to control the masses, as you can see.

Nevertheless, lets get back to the beauty of water and consider what a magnificently supportive being it is. It is the blood of our planet, containing the memories of the universe, running through the tributaries and falling from the sky, never traveling in a straight line, endlessly renewing its vibrancy.

By subjecting water to vortices, we can recalibrate the negative program of a compromised liquid crystal and return it to a positive state. The same effect can be achieved within the human physiology, through the art of *Lo Ban Pai*[viii], my movement system that augments one's absorption of photons into the fluid structure of the body. The spiraling vortices created by the movements become internally activated through practice, revitalizing internal reservoirs with optimal photonic potential.

Water will always transform in comparison to what is necessary within its environment. It is the most intensely empathic entity on this planet, and it is vibrantly moving within us. Even though it is obviously operating from an alternate phylum, we are more than symbiotically connected. We are water that walks and talks.

Every intention, even a flower placed in water, alters its living reality through the absorption of that vibration. In

---

[viii] See www.parallelperception.com for more information on Lo Ban Pai.

homeopathic medicine it has been discovered that if a petal of a rose is put into a vial of water, the crystalline structure will morph to emulate the frequency obtained from that petal. Roses are well known for their ability to cool the heart when it is overheated, simply through an infusion of pure petals made into tea.

The Chinese have known the power of herbs in all forms and have applied these natural medicines since time immemorial. It is only the onset of new technology that gives confirmation to the fact that water will change through contact with anything that is placed within it, or even near it. Our world is extremely complex.

As for beyond our planetary situation, similar rules apply. The way universal communion naturally occurs is not too dissimilar to the experience I had with the water spirit in terms of empathic absorption. Even though we are from different phylums, through osmosis information is obtained. Whether this import is valuable or detrimental to one's being will define itself as one proceeds. On most occasions, the clarity of the exchange depends on withholding one's need to assume that their bias is correct.

We are in a constant state of reception. We are being shifted and redefined through that calibration in every moment, in every circumstance, whether we realize it or not. As we journey through our universe, each star emanates a particular frequency that can be felt and absorbed by every being on this planet.

How strange it is to see light coming from the sky at night, and how beautiful it is to gaze upon the light of the sun illuminating the face of the moon.

This reminds me of an old saying about chopping wood and carrying water. The metaphor states that, no matter who you are, in winter you have to chop wood and all year you must carry water. In observing this universal axiom, consider this, when you bear a bucket of water, is it an illusion that you see the reflection of the moon shining within it?

Water is a very powerful element. The moon is actually more than in the bucket. The water has absorbed its information. The true illusion is the bias that surrounds the reflection, and the idea that the bucket does not contain it. There are many things that we don't understand yet. For example, how do we begin to fathom bias when it is the reflection of our reality being shone back to us, as the moon appearing within the water?

Our belief systems are caught in a very strange gridlock of illusions that we deem real. There are many reflections on our planet in terms of different species that convey to us who we are and how we are caught. Yet, when I relay this story to you, which way will you see it? Let's proceed.

There was once a fisherman who had brought his trawler home to port. He had caught some crabs to be sold at the market in the early hours of the morning, and as he was securing his vessel on the dock, a young man passed by, noticing that he had a large crate full of exotic crabs without any lid to contain them. Seeing that hundreds of them could potentially climb out, he asked the fisherman, "Aren't your crabs going to escape if you don't cover them?"

The trawler owner replied, "There is no need for a lid. Many species of crab have a very strange habit. If one tries to climb out, three or four of the crabs around it will grab its legs and stop it from reaching the top. They all do this. Every one of them."

The fishermen winked at the young man, "Pretty strange behavior, hey?" he said, and continued about his business.

With this tale about the behavior of crabs what I am attempting to convey is that, as human beings in a state of profound cognitive dissonance, we fail to realize that with our bias - no matter how diverse or multi-culturally defined - we hold each other fixed from escaping into new and interesting perspectives via the collective, fixed intent of humanity at large.

If a person were to state, two hundred years ago, "When you focus on water it will change via your influence, and then that water will become your intention", they would have been burned at the stake as a witch for blasphemy.

Yet we evolve and progress, still hounded by our bias, even though we are always moving through new phases in our development. Which in essence begs the question: Are we really evolving with the appropriate speed that necessitates the changes that must occur on a planetary scale at this time?

Suggestions, assumptions, bias, are like an incantation. A spell cast without a wand being employed. Now you may wonder, in true earnest, what this has to do with the appearance of the disappearing?

I would like to assure you that I am getting there nice and slowly. Very gently I want you to see what I have discovered on the arduous journey called life. I will relay one more story here before I go back to the three containers and the magic of water.

This is an experience I had at around the age of twenty-seven. I had my own clinic and did Oriental body work, very similar to how medical massage is practiced in Beijing hospital, and on occasion I would hold treatment sessions in alternative clinics.

It was very demanding work and required an enormous amount of energy to perform it correctly. You need to be so attuned that you can feel the maladies within the organs of the people you treat, so as to work appropriately upon the meridian lines of the body. This requires that the practitioner be sensitive enough to intuit their patient's situation via the feeling that emanates from their client's body, in correlation with a physical assessment that includes facial, tongue and pulse diagnosis.

We won't travel any further on the path of Chinese medicine beyond this point. I would prefer to stay with the realizations of an empath and reveal how the blood - every single cell - is autonomously aware of its own existence; and simultaneously is co-opted into an enormous faction of communal conductivity that collects itself into the center of the toroidal field of our physical form. This location is the heart chakra.

In the body of a fully functioning empath, one begins to know things irrefutably. It is within the whole physiology that the seer receives information. Every cell emanates energy that bursts forwards as photonic potential, which becomes the spiraling vortices of the toroidal field.

On one occasion when I was working in an alternate medical clinic, I had to share a room with another practitioner. To my chagrin, this person was very bossy and controlling. I would be reprimanded terribly if I moved one item an inch out of its place. I wondered how she could possibly be working in this field with such innate hostility. I did my best not to move a thing, but was always very uncomfortable in her presence.

After many years of study, she obtained her osteopathic license and decided to open her own clinic. As a gesture of encouragement I said that I'd love to come and support her in her new endeavor in life.

A few months later I made an appointment to go and see her about a strange thing I had occurring in my calves; a constant muscular flicking that is called fasciculation. It was a result of training six hours a day of the art of Lo Ban Pai, and also getting up at three o-clock in the morning to practice meditation and yoga.

At this stage I had been committed to this yogic discipline for about ten years. I was obviously deficient in certain vital minerals and electrolytes as a result of all the training that I was doing. I was young and strong and ignoring what I needed to do with my diet.

Upon arrival to her clinic she informed me that she had a live blood analysis microscope, and during the session she asked if she could obtain some of my blood for observation. She proceeded to prick my thumb and put a drop of my blood in between two small rectangular frames of glass. She popped it under the microscope and said, "You seem to be very healthy. Your blood is not clumping. Let's have a closer look."

When she leaned in to do so, we both got the shock of our life. Before I tell you why, so that you have a clear picture of what I am going to describe, have you ever watched a documentary where a herd of gazelle are approached by a helicopter and they run in a defined group, all in the same direction away from that disturbance, trying to escape what they perceive as a predator?

When the naturopath looked into the microscope at my blood, it fled from her gaze, away from her body that was approaching. She looked up at me, completely taken aback. She didn't know what was happening, but I knew immediately what had occurred. I looked at her calmly and said, "My blood doesn't like you. I can't proceed with this appointment." In those days I didn't talk very much. I simply left the room and never saw her again.

This is how the blood functions in the physiology of an empath, as I was to discover on that fateful day. Beyond that point in time, I always trusted my body when I knew I needed to get out of the proximity of somebody who was dangerous for me. Now let's return to the story of the three containers and discover why this information is valuable for all of us.

Lotus Floating Over Muddy Waters

The most challenging thing to understand within the element of emptiness is that it sits in close proximity to an all-encompassing being that is available within every moment, yet seemingly unavailable, since we cannot notice it by utilizing our present-day cognitive system, which is limiting us through the binding power of our collective bias.

From a quantum perspective, physicists have established that at the basis of everything that upholds our reality, nothing appears. There is simply a vibratory force that emanates the corresponding frequency that allows each element that is visually comprehensible to appear directly in front of all of us as a form. That manifestation will then be echoed within every human being's consciousness once it is seen and understood for what it is, via our unified capacity to see.

To give a visual reference to what I am describing, imagine a flower as it falls from a tree, spiraling until it sits weightlessly upon the ground. All of us, if we were observing this phenomenon, would recognize that this understanding replicates itself through our perception. At the basis of that creation there is an omnipresent factor that holds the physical form of that flower in place with the tension of the sound frequency that resonates from within it.

Yet even those working in the most advanced fields of current day physics still don't comprehend the crux of this principle. The question remains: How can there be nothing creating something for us to witness?

As you can see from this brief description, we all hold the beauty of a flower within the reverence of its appearance. From its emptiness it has created a feeling within us, and we all simultaneously cooperate with what has been absorbed. Remember though, the essence of what we perceive is always affected by our bias and what we believe to be absolute as a truth in comparison to our experience.

What we haven't fully taken into account as a humanity is that we are enthralled by an internal dialogue that possesses us from within, as we have already discussed in the chapter of *The Ghost.*

It is very difficult to apprehend what is meant to be internally witnessed when it is not obviously apparent, and this is a direct result of being trained not to be aware of it. Here we discover the most disturbing paradox, which will be exemplified throughout this text.

Individuals become possessed by their own thought forms, and I deliberately use the term *possession* in the context of being unknown to oneself via the fact that something else has taken over when the internal dialogue positions itself to be in command.

You would ask yourself: What has this got to do with the

three containers experiment, of highly acclaimed Japanese scientist, Dr. Emoto? As you will soon see, it has got everything to do with his study, and we will move through this very carefully, so that everyone may fully comprehend how synchronistically these subjects relate.

I have begun the explanation of the three containers of rice by using the example of the third jar first: the one that was ignored. We will strip this down into its vital components so that you can understand what it means to be absently available and then disregard what needs to be noticed, via the fact that never being introduced to an element breeds a very strange ignorance of that factor.

How can you discover something that you are not familiar with? The dilemma that we are facing within humanity as a whole is that we were programmed to look elsewhere, rather than become aware of that ubiquitous presence that inevitably will awaken our intuitive empath from within.

Our journey is to become acquainted with that which makes itself available, and we must understand that identifying rising and falling elements as *good* and *bad* within our perception has created an abnormal internal dissonance. We will eventually come back to the favored jar, and the jar that was filled with contempt. Both are an intention that requires a corresponding belief system to acquire a result.

Now let's look at the alteration of perception from a different perspective. Yesterday, my student, Daniela, said to me, "Lujan, what we have realized by being with you is of immense value to us, but we don't understand the term shamanism, or shaman."

Shamanism, in connection with *you,* primarily means the altering of one's perception towards the ultimate truth: A path with heart. There are many dissonant connotations that are connected with these terms. In other words, subtexts that can be ascribed in comparison to a person focusing their bias or belief system upon the act of identifying with something in order to acquire personal power.

Throughout my last four publications I have endeavored to deal with the truth and enlightenment of the journey of one who wishes to alter their perception to become enhanced by a path with heart, and to actively withdraw from subterfuge of any kind. The hidden subtext of a craft that requires behavior that steers one's essence away from the integrity one is wishing to embody must be revealed and dissolved for real progress to occur.

The only reason that I will entertain the subject of shamanism beyond this point is that it is directly related with one of my primary teachers, Juan Matus. He was a pure, intuitive empath, as the following revelations upon the abstract cores of his teachings will reveal. My motivation here is to eradicate the perceptual bias that is acquainted with the word shamanism and undo the damage that has been done.

My students have inquisitively inquired as to how I become recalibrated via my circumstances, so as to adapt to each new practitioner who comes to learn Lo Ban Pai. The following explanation will directly deal with the misconception of the onlooker and illustrate how I operate as an intuitive empath.

I will open the door to a Toltec teaching, to provide an example of why it is so important not to have an internal dialogue and to establish the understanding that we are ignoring something that can easily be comprehended. But first we must experience it through conceiving of it as a possibility.

Juan Matus was a very powerful individual. I have described his presence within my own life, appearing in parallel timelines within alternate dream visions. His name within *The Art of Stalking Parallel Perception*, before he was revealed, was Zakai.

I have learnt many things by example, and I have intended to live my life to reflect that living experience that was transmitted. I am bound by a vow to open all possible doors so the world that I was introduced to as a child can be completely understood by those who come in contact with me.

I have realized that doing and explaining what one is doing is very important. One can be taught through language, and the transmission of feeling through that communication. One can also learn by witnessing the actions of another, but if the internal dialogue is relentlessly present, many things will be missed.

In the chapter of *The Ghost* we looked at how the upper center, the mind, is meant to be empty. It is constantly listening, and continually experiencing the tactile senses through inward recognition. It witnesses the ebbs and flows of the internal currents of the body as feeling, and patiently waits for the heart to speak through the mechanisms of a transmission of sound frequency that cannot be heard but can be felt intensely.

The book of life, my existence, your lifetime, sits patiently to be read by your own words that are generated by internal wisdom to arise and be spoken. It is a mindful awaiting, not full of thoughts but ever-presently witnessing from a void-like state, from the command center where the third eye is stationed.

I am describing the empty mind's true ability to perceive. With sufficient introspection a person can begin to understand what cannot be understood. Bear with these contradictions. They are truths that will realize themselves within you through your own experiences. Now on to a well-known Toltec story that was relayed in *Journey to Ixtlan* by Carlos Castaneda, to reveal that which is hidden within those pages.

On one occasion when Juan Matus was with his apprentice, he suddenly snatched the keys from his hands and threw them into the chaparral, to Castaneda's chagrin and disbelief. Looking aghast at his teacher, he asked him why he would do such a thing, becoming immediately offended and confused.

This is the emotional bias of not understanding what is happening and it was this barrier that Juan Matus was revealing to him about his behavior. Being offended recalibrates all the water and blood to coalesce into a concentrated point of dissonance, and this was his misunderstanding of what was truly meant to be understood.

Castaneda proceeded to search for the keys, zigzagging through the grass, trying to discover where they had landed. However, his emotionality had blocked his true feeling, obscuring his innate ability to internally realize what needed to be known.

Juan Matus very patiently called to him, "Come and sit down and forget about your emotions. When you stop being offended your body will relax. Sit with me quietly. Don't think about what I have done. Wait for your body to know what it needs to do."

At this stage of his apprenticeship, Juan Matus was dealing with Carlos' body consciousness, and knew that he had a really big problem with emotions and an unrelenting internal dialogue. Snatching the keys from him to disrupt his expectations was one of the methods he used to trigger his self-importance to come to the surface.

After about three quarters of an hour of relaxing, forgetting about what Juan Matus had done, Carlos' unruly emotions had disappeared and his body knew exactly where the keys were. He stood up within that realization, walked straight to where they had fallen and picked them up.

The true man appeared at this point, and what had disappeared was the illusion of the man who he *was*. The disappearing of the appearing, in a state of reversal.

On a cellular level, he irrefutably knew what to do. He had absorbed an enormous amount of personal power from being in contact with Juan Matus, in essence borrowing momentarily what was necessary to show him how to proceed with his life.

The next element I will introduce demonstrates how an

empath truly operates from their empty command center, and will illustrate clearly how I am recalibrated by my students to reveal a combination of movement that belongs to that moment and is a result of their influence upon my being, which in essence is a gift to everyone present.

Our neurological processing relies upon a synaptic system which fires electromagnetic signals from one receptor site to another in a network that resembles the roots of a plant. The best way to illustrate this firing process is that it looks like when lightening strikes from its origin to its destination. It appears and disappears, momentarily.

Within this vast connective tapestry, the power of repetition creates an intelligence that becomes self-aware within the spiraling vortexes it travels upon, thus commanding the body to move via its innate receptivity.

For example, within the practice of internal kung fu, the more familiar you become, the more power is acquired, through a network of electrical impulses which create magnetism, or gravity, within the field of one's toroidal essence.

If I have been practicing a form for forty years, alternate neural pathways have developed within my empty command center. I have also obtained a corresponding effect of symbiotic cooperation that renders my movements full of power. I am familiar absolutely with that and this accumulation of energy is transferred to my students through their diligent application toward this devotion.

It must be understood at this point that the repetition that is required for the body to obtain power is not the same momentum that is acquired through the repetitious mind that talks to itself.

Reason is extremely limited, and can be manipulated if we are focused on the wrong things. For instance, on a path that does not resonate with the purpose of our true destiny. Self-actualization cannot be achieved through thinking. It can only be attained through the simplicity of pure action.

Coming back to Carlos Castaneda and the abstract cores found within his writings, let's look at what happened next to discover how the internal dialogue interferes with what really can be known through its dogged insistence within habitual pathways.

Carlos Castaneda was sitting with Juan Matus on the verandah of his ramshackle cabin. Carlos was very confused about how he had known what to do in terms of retrieving the keys from the chaparral.

He realized that he had found something that couldn't really be located in a normal way. He had followed a feeling that was so obscure and non-concrete that even when he picked up the keys he still didn't understand how he had acquired this ability by stopping doing what he was doing.

Through his reasoning, he was trying to fathom what had occurred, and a question formed in his mind. "If there was a man, 500 yards away from your front door, with a rifle that had a telescopic sight aimed at you, intent on assassination, what would you do?" he asked.

"While the man is there, I simply wouldn't go out my front door," Juan Matus replied calmly. "I would leave and enter through the back. I just wouldn't make myself available. If my personal power is strong, I would listen to the conviction of my body and follow it irrefutably."

This story has been very hard for people to understand in terms of its deeper meaning. It has woven within it the concept of being accessible and inaccessible. Juan Matus is saying: I simply will not be available for the rifleman to aim at me, so I will not appear where he wants me to be.

What he didn't reveal is how an intruder's presence would become accessible to him. How this occurs and how an empty mind can be mindful was never explained nor examined for what it truly is. Juan Matus is referring to being recalibrated to respond in a way that is infused with what appears to be abstract magic, filled with personal power.

It is difficult for an empath to elucidate an unseen process, but now we are collectively advanced enough to conceive of new possibilities through the advent of quantum physics, which has given the ways and means to convey what really takes place in a circumstance like this.

When the mind is empty, void of any thoughts, it is adaptive and pliable. We utilize a system of synaptic roots, which are fibers of energy that conduct light from one neuron to another to fire as a command to direct the body on what to do and what not to do.

This process, whilst an ever-present reality, is so obscure that it escapes comprehension. We are going to bridge that gap today, and define how a network of light filaments – our collective synapses – fill the air as electrical currents all around us in a fourth dimensional electromagnetic grid of connective intelligence, which looks like a haystack composed of luminous fibers that seem to be random within their placement.

Emitting and receiving endless frequencies simultaneously, it mirrors what it becomes aware of within a fractal refraction that reflects the components of the empty mind into the spaces in between things.

Even though those factors are seemingly void of substance, they contain the quality of their own individuality through the frequency they generate, which in actuality is innumerable in comparison to the momentary effect of one element residing within the presence of another; and this is simultaneity within its full expression.

The most challenging thing to comprehend is that one frequency, which may be 20 hertz, can travel along a light fiber in the opposite direction to a 500 hertz frequency upon the very same filament, creating an immediate communication between points of origin whereby each recognizes the sound emitted, instantaneously.

In other words, there is no time lapse between the signal and the reception, and even though two different messages are both traveling on the same pathway they retain their unique signature, only transforming upon the catalytic point of reception from both sides, thus indicating that the locus must adapt to the new import of sensory data. This interchange can occur transdimensionally, and also between similar constructs on different timelines, and can equally encompass alternate lifetime continuums.

If we use the example of a string being plucked on a guitar, our rigid view in terms of this understanding is that two sounds cannot be played on one string at the same time, and here lies our cognitive dissonance; our inability to understand the fluidity of the truth that is already there.

Our compulsion to identify something as one or the other – our bias – neutralizes the fluid sphere of possibility that allows perception of all states simultaneously. This is the quantum superposition in terms of awareness.

As many people have affirmed, we are all one. Yet it is not enough to say this alone. We have to understand *how* we are all one, and why have we forgotten and subsequently ignored what is in plain sight in deference to our programming.

The interconnective filaments of light are internally stationed, observing the essence of themselves within the human organism and everywhere else simultaneously. What prevents us from consciously acknowledging what is "impossible" to realize is our prejudice: our bias. And these blinding filters are continually reaffirmed, over and over again, via emotions that become reliably triggered by the internal dialogue.

In other words, we must come to terms with the root of our emotional dysfunction through understanding why it is happening, and know that our mind is like a computer that has inserted within it a viral Trojan horse that directs it away from what it is meant to do.

The corrupted script that steals our true moment only serves the purpose of the social engineers who have mindfully cultivated the perfection of our collective confusion through trial and error over time.

Imagine inside the empty mind of Juan Matus, sitting in his cabin. Let's say that the frequency his biofield is emitting is 7.83 hertz. The neural network of his silent command center fires in recognition of a dissonant frequency, which is the intent to cause harm - for instance 55 hertz - that is firing within the rifleman's neural network. Remember, this is the superposition in action.

Juan Matus wouldn't recognize this rationally, but his body would know it intuitively and will proceed to take the right course of action. The information from his empty command center sends a neural signal as an electrical impulse to change the directive of his body not to be available at that particular point, since danger is looming. This is how the internal process of an empath operates. One is recalibrated.

The catalytic effect occurs in Juan Matus' realizations via the twin factor, in terms of recognition of the invisible filaments of light connecting the empty mind to the spaces in between two points of origin. One is operating from the socially engineered script, and the other is free of that engineering.

What would happen after this point is that Juan Matus would probably go out his back door, circle around the ridge, come upon the gunman from behind and upon that arrival instantaneously realize why he didn't walk out the front door. This is how perceptual calibration occurs from an empathic perspective.

A similar process takes place between my students and myself. When familiar movements that I have practiced all my life are disrupted to do something different, it is because the neural network of the one witnessing has beckoned my body to notice and adapt in comparison to the person that is right in front of me.

An empath is recalibrated by every advent, and this is how

my students diagnose their own energetics through my emptiness. Thus we proceed with a set of movements that are sequenced in a new way, designed specifically for that person or group of people. This is the adaptive, growth principle of the internal workings of an intuitive empath. The last container is a very elusive element to comprehend.

Dr. Emoto has stumbled upon the mystery of all mysteries in terms of our evolution as empaths. This interconnective factor is why we must be of service to everything that appears before our path. Not to judge, nor to favor, but simply witness so that we can appropriately be recalibrated through this technique.

The abyss, the emptiness, is profoundly overwhelming. We have been taught to ignore it, and our lives are becoming like a wretched swamp. We must endeavor to communally realize how interconnected we really are, through not expecting to discover anything. This is the mechanism of how to intuit seeing.

Patiently waiting without expectation is a fundamental key to this entry point of reality, which is only as real as the subtleties that unveil themselves to you on your journey of being revealed. This is the art of proceeding with not really knowing how to proceed, until it becomes apparent in the moment that is continually escaping you.

The primary foundation of this receptive state of being requires you not to have an internal dialogue. You must be *exactly* who you are meant to be and stop trying to be anybody. To truly be somebody you must give up every holding that binds you to who you think you are.

The subject of ignoring is immense. Are we blissfully ignorant of the fact that we have been taught to disregard what is truly our path as spiritual beings? We have acquired this disharmonious state through the first two containers. You are *good,* and you are *bad.*

To return to an earlier parallel, the Toltec path and shamanism can potentially harbor many subtexts, and these are just as dangerous as the man hiding in the bushes with a gun. These self-identifying concepts foster bias via labyrinthine eddies within the consciousness of those who wish to cultivate personal power through methods gained via hearsay instead of personal experience.

As you can see, these skills cannot be forcibly acquired. They simply manifest by turning off your Trojan horse - your internal dialogue and unwholesome expectations - and then what appears will always be one hundred percent unexpected. There our destiny awaits us. That is why I don't subscribe to anything other than what is immediately presenting itself. Here is where one must be truly available, and act appropriately.

THE QUANTUM PARADOX

Throughout all the explanations concerning the container that has been ignored, many aspects of the preferred jar and the condemned jar have also been elucidated quite extensively. If you read carefully you will notice this.

What I would now like to draw your awareness toward is the duplicitous nature of the idea of *good* and *bad*, and how this dualistic aspect of our attention has seized upon the false idea that our behavioral patterns can be virtuous and condemning simultaneously.

Step-by-step, I want you to see that dissonance within our

self-reflection can lead us to believe that we can justify everything we do, based upon the premise of an internal reflection that will faithfully condone every step taken.

The most challenging thing to realize when one attempts to grow through what is besetting our present consciousness is the fact that our cognitive bias creates a membrane that distances us from the reality of what is occurring as a result of our actions.

I would like to open your horizons towards such potential consequences via some stories that will reveal the astonishing impact that one element can have upon another, without us being aware of these possibilities.

Within Dr. Emoto's labs, many things were discovered, both by chance and by trial and error. Observing the effects of happenstance is so enlightening. Enormous insights may come upon an inquirer unexpectedly, brought to light through mere accident. Or is it?

Within the elemental structure of the alchemy of our world, whatever we focus upon avails itself to us. And hiding one thing eventually reveals another, as you will see.

Within the *accident* it is often the concealed element that uncovers what is cloaked. Is this a part of the personality of the individual being brought to the surface? I am asking myself whether this inquiry was ever made within the story that follows.

In one of the labs where Dr. Emoto's experimentations upon water took place, there was a colleague conducting an experiment with a vial of poison. Whilst transporting this toxic material in a hermetically sealed glass, moving it from one part of the room to another, this scientist somehow became preoccupied and dropped it into a beaker of water.

They attempted to remove it immediately but the neck of the container was too narrow to access by hand. Their day must have been terribly busy and this colleague became involved in another task, which allowed them to forget about retrieving the vial. Whether this was an accident or a mistake is not really the point, but the results were astounding.

As it turned out, this water was the fluid that they gave to the mice to keep them hydrated. Twenty-four hours or so passed, and the mice needed to be looked after. Their water was replenished from this container and to everybody's shock and dismay they all died.

Subsequent tests showed that the toxins that had killed them displayed the symptoms of that poison, yet there was no actual residue of it in the blood of the dead mice. The substance in the vial had no way to bleed into the clean water. That was an irrefutable fact. What they all eventually realized was that the vibratory signature of the contaminant had recalibrated the water that surrounded it.

This leads me to a very old saying: "It only takes one bad apple to ruin the whole barrel".

An infection or transmission of an effect can proliferate itself, not only through contact but also via the potency of its intended vibration into the environment, as demonstrated by the fact of the poison recalibrating the clean water to its memory.

Within itself this story is extraordinary, but there is one other aspect that we must examine, and it has to do with the content of human behavior.

Quite often when I am teaching, I ask my students to

revert to their lowest common denominator so they can deal with who they really are instead of pretending to be someone they are not.

If one is aware of the worst feeling that one is not proud of, and yet pretends to be something else or convinces themselves that the image they are projecting is wholesome and good and therefore renders their compromise undetectable, then one is suffering a very strange illusion in terms of not taking responsibility for that malady residing within.

We first have to deal with the underlying disruption before we can be truly happy and content with who we are. Otherwise the jarring discord that surrounds what has been surreptitiously avoided and intentionally concealed will have repercussions upon every circumstance until the root cause of the dysfunction has had a light shined upon it.

There is an enormous amount of energy that goes into shame and self-blame, and these elements must be addressed before one proceeds on the path of service to others. We must begin by becoming of service to ourselves by uprooting the bad seed that wishes to grow amidst the crop of goodness within. In this extract from the Bible we find reference to this from another point of view.

Matthew 13:24-43, The Parable of Weeds among the Wheat.

The kingdom of heaven may be compared to someone who sowed good seed in his field; but while everybody was asleep, an enemy came and sowed weeds among the wheat, and then went away.

So when the plants came up and bore grain, then the weeds appeared as well. And the servants of the householder came and said to him, "Master, did you not sow good seed in your field? Where, then, did these weeds come from?" He answered, "An enemy has done this."

The servants said to him, "Then do you want us to go and gather them?" But he replied, "No; for in gathering the weeds you would uproot the wheat along with them. Let both of them grow together until the harvest; and at harvest time I will tell the reapers, Collect the weeds first and bind them in bundles to be burned, but gather the wheat into my barn."

The reason I include this here is that Yeshua, the seer commonly known as Jesus, was an intuitive empath. There is a very interesting detail within this parable that hasn't really been given due attention.

The strategy behind the weeds not being pulled out early is that, metaphorically, it is better to observe the enemy as they intend to grow roots and bear fruit in a circumstance. This way you can fully comprehend the tactics that have been applied within the depths of a surreptitious intent towards a wholesome situation.

As one patiently observes the machinations of an adversary, one becomes gradually enlightened in terms of the dangers of the world that surround us. Before the enemy's tactics come to full fruition, the seeds they have sown are uprooted and burnt, thereby protecting the good intentions from harm, as portrayed in the story of the wheat not being interfered with until it is fully-grown. But there are also subtexts to take into consideration.

If the unwholesome strategies that were observed are replicated as a tactic in future circumstances under the guise of goodness by the one who has noticed them, then virtue is lost within the depths of sin, and the owner of the property becomes no different to the enemy. His intentions would then take on the unethical characteristics of those who he had observed previously.

Here we see that the discipline of detachment and humility within self-reflective service are necessary hallmarks of an empathic view. Otherwise one becomes subject to an internal dissent that will occupy a frequency of discord that may be difficult to recover from. Such a state is compounded by the fact that this intent hides behind a white hat, which in actuality has become black through corrupt application.

To deepen the understanding of sin and to help lever it out of its religious context, this term refers to the act of applying oneself incorrectly. The opposite of sin is essentially a method of feeling what can be applied without disturbing the sovereign nature of one's rapture of the heart, which attempts to be continually on the path of ascension.

In other words, one begins to realize that there is a right and wrong way to proceed so that one does not fall into a dissonant frequency in terms of vexing this sacred center's harmonious equilibrium.

If we now reverse a little bit and go back to the lab, we can draw another insight to the surface. That vial may have been dropped into the water accidentally and then hidden from view because the person didn't want to be discovered. Then the water was given to the mice and upon this event a cascade of circumstances occurred, revealing their studies from another perspective.

The poison became an absolute reflection of the actions of that scientist who didn't want to be seen as someone who had made a simple mistake. In other words, this individual may not have wanted their error to be discovered, which is tantamount to intending another's eyes to overlook what had been done. This is comparable to the container that had been intentionally ignored, which is a very strange paradox.

Here I would like you to realize that intending your

companions not to see what has occurred is employing the strategy of the container that had been willfully disregarded, via directing others not to see.

This is the black hat influencing a situation through intention. Instead of resulting in a wretched smell, withholding that information had fatal consequences for the mice. That one gesture revealed a nefarious fractality, even though the original intent was not in place for such an outcome to occur. And that's what the container of ignoring has prompted us to observe.

At this point I would like to direct your eyes to see how an honest mistake became something else when the intention to hide was added. Within the air of pure observation, a worldwide situation has been revealed in the simple actions of someone within a laboratory.

Was the water teaching us what is really occurring? Frequencies or vibrations cannot be hidden from view, and when we see this situation for what it is, it becomes a metaphorical tool for learning.

This is a pure parallel to dropping your covert behaviors

into the appearance of the goodness of your actions that you wish to reveal to others, whilst hoping you will not be seen for who you really are. In essence this is masquerading as somebody you are not, just as the water turned out to be different than what the scientists expected, with grave consequences upon other living beings.

Here we arrive upon another strange paradox inherent within the containment field of our bias. Dr. Emoto *intended* to ignore the third container, which in actuality is not the same as not interfering with something that one is not aware of.

This brings into question the outcome of the study, in terms of a fundamental contradiction that we may easily overlook because of our subjectivity. The way this manifests in this case is that he is an authority in his field and we are not. Very interesting, isn't it, how this might slip by unnoticed. Have you realized?

As you put this together, I would now like to relay another story about water, and how it can appear to be different to what it really is. I would like you to be totally aware that I am using these narratives to reflect upon behavior that may be covertly hidden behind the mask of goodness.

There were a group of Asian businessmen who were destroying the landscape of a particular region, poisoning the rivers and streams of the surrounding area. They were more interested in making profit than in taking responsibility for the results of their actions upon the lands.

There was a lot of resentment from the locals towards them, and whenever they had meetings in the areas where they were profiteering, they would never eat food during their sessions, and would always test the water before drinking it to make sure it was safe.

On this particular day, they proceeded with their meeting as usual and drank the water that was brought to them, which they had been informed was fine. Upon awakening in the early hours of the next morning, they were all suffering severe food poisoning and could not comprehend how their situation had been infiltrated.

Somebody had known about how to intend something to be *good,* and simultaneously *bad,* and they had altered the water by concentrating the intent: *You are poisonous but nobody will notice,* upon its crystalline structure. In essence this procured the same results as the vial containing deadly poison that was accidentally dropped into the mice's drinking water.

Here I would like you to look very carefully at the picture I am painting. To progress on our paths as empaths, one cannot entertain any negativity. There is nowhere to proceed until the root of disharmony has been pulled from the fertile soil of one's consciousness, so as to reap the benefits of a pure, good harvest, which is one's life to be witnessed, as nourishment, and the power contained within after the consumption.

The Rapture

By becoming genuinely acquainted with the subjectivity of our illusions we can understand that they are in essence our confirmation bias. Once we realize this, our attention will turn towards something else that may be unfamiliar, until we are able to recognize it as the rapture arising within.

The rapture is a feeling that travels up the center of the chest, rises through the throat and offers the sacred scriptures of the heart to be spoken. You are looking at what can't be viewed, you are verbalizing what has never been heard, you are listening to what you are saying, and you become a conduit, an absolute reflection of the living essence of your environment. This is a natural function of an empathic human being, or an earthling.

You witness the rapture and faithfully follow the scriptures of your own insightful realizations in the context of what is being revealed within the sacredness of that empty moment. You feel the momentum of what you know yet it has got nothing to do with you and everything to do with what you've received.

Whenever empathic exchange occurs, the heart will immediately interpret through the excitement of communication. You hear what you are saying but you have no idea what the essential elements of what you are going to convey will be. The other person, or the field of energy that's transmitting their vibratory essence within you, enters your internal beingness to be witnessed and then you automatically assign words to that recalibration.

If there is no content within that sphere of exchange the empath will leave the circumstance or wait patiently for the moment to release them. You will know there is no point in pursuing that communication by the fact that there is no receptivity. Upon the realization that you can't proceed any further you must withdraw the magic of your words, for the essential capacity of that moment isn't capable of attuning to the frequency being sent.

Just imagine that you have two tuning forks. One has been struck and is vibrating and the corresponding fork in close proximity will begin to vibrate with the same frequency. This is how empaths communicate, whether another individual realizes it is happening or not.

The insistent non-availability of human beings to be recalibrated to the natural ebbs and flows of the world around them at this present time in history has mainly to do with not believing that we can be something more than what we are.

When the arising emanation, which becomes the empath's vital communication, is interrupted by the non-availability of the moment at large, the general rule of thumb is to observe without bias.

If the moment becomes available to be spoken to, through articulating the essential essence of that rapture, one will listen to what has never been heard or mentioned before, within the context of being subject to an unfamiliar feeling that immediately becomes recognizable through empathic attunement.

This relates to *being, knowing* and *not-doing,* as outlined in *Whisperings of the Dragon.* This subtle dynamic of exchange is the symbiotic process of an empath who is operating harmoniously. In an environment where there is no other person you will be subject to the same natural laws.

You will head in a certain direction and you will have no idea why. Instead of going to the right, you walk left. Your body will lead you. This is the same process that occurs when you see and don't judge another person.

The first discipline is to witness and not formulate an opinion. Trust that your body will do the most appropriate thing. If at this point you begin to talk to yourself about what is happening this is not being empathic, and may cause you to second-guess yourself.

The most pure approach you can adopt is to notice exactly what you are observing, and sincerely attempt not to limit or hold circumstances within a perceptual boundary, for this may evolve into a reflective intolerance.

We must allow others to traverse without the weight of our perception restricting them. Realize that it is an evolutionary imperative to not fall into the trap of well-worn behavioral patterns, for a habitual response is a sign that your empathic attunement is out of alignment.

You must cultivate the discipline of detachment; to know what you see and then not digress into congratulating yourself about what you've noticed. Take what you've witnessed as the lowest common denominator, put it behind you, and then watch how that agenda develops without interfering with it.

When you do that you can actually see where the mistake of someone else's life wishes to take you, for you are mindfully observing a circumstance without adding yourself to it.

Being mindful doesn't mean to think about what is happening. It means being empty. There's a big difference between having a skull riddled with thoughts and a mind full of emptiness.

An awareness infused with silence will listen to the rapture of the heart, absorbing and expressing that uprising feeling as a conduit of eternity. This universal axiom requires the ears to be one hundred percent externally bound, awaiting for information to be relayed within pertinent fields of communication. We become receptive to the endless echoes of emptiness conveying something from nothing.

We all must be aware that the quality of antimatter does not emit a recognizable frequency to be witnessed by the human organism. This is why the principle of being nobody is so important to understand. A humble perspective can speak the wisdom that appears from the eternal abyss, by virtue of its non-insistence upon a bias.

Remember to be mindfully observant to the advent of your own voice arising to offer unknown content, in terms of your compassion and your service to the circumstance that is confronting you. That is a true empath's journey, and everybody who wishes to be empathically attuned must endeavor to emulate these subtleties.

To quote terminology from *Whisperings of the Dragon,*

remember that your eyes are only employed as a two percent cursory glance at the world around you; yet you are fully impacted through their impressions since they are feeling ninety-eight percent of the circumstance being gazed upon within that internal recognition. This in turn will rearrange the perception of one's heart to be delivered to the awareness of a precognitive communication that becomes available within one's full attention.

Whilst the eyes are primarily looking at what has arrived within, that two percent of external visual focus is actually locating what needs to be spoken to, through the auspice of that transmission. In other words, one's awareness is occupying many viable points as the empathic superposition, for it retains no fixed standpoint but receives pertinent material via that exchange.

Now let's revert back to the visual anomaly of strands of light falling from infinite space, that reveal a haystack of fibers which are intelligently organized, and will catalyze the point of origin upon the realization of any pressure becoming available.

This absolutely relates to what is known as the Mandela Effect, which alters the content of timelines through an intimate infusion of fractalization, and a state of potentiality that implies that personal objectivity can be shifted and changed via an arbitrary constant.

In other words, whatever we do has repercussions, which in turn will relay that transformation back to each source of its initial intention in multiples. Not unlike ripples from a pebble dropped in a pond, the reverberations of our awareness are endlessly returning to their origins to be reorganized.

The mainstay of empathic communication is derived from connecting to those light fibers that carry infinite potential for transmission. Whichever frequency that one is focused upon can simultaneously receive another vibration that has alternate information contained within.

Thus we are progressively aligned by the present reception becoming available, whilst concurrently being momentarily attuned *offsite* by a frequency that can't be read via the fact that our phylum cannot directly interpret this field of potentiality. And even if we imagine we could, this universal aspect would not cooperate, for the bias of our perception invariably interferes with that subtlety.

Since we are being recalibrated by a phylum that we can't recognize via our social engineering, we must wait patiently to recapitulate that which is awaiting to be experienced. Our unbiased observation of what has arrived from an unknown field of origin is our empty potential revealing itself to be witnessed. This is the result of the infusion of one's essence being influenced by anti-matter.

We can refer to this realm of perception as God consciousness, but it is much more than that. Its very nature is beyond imagination. This is the vital juncture of realization that collapses the bias of the previous vibration where attention had been held.

If you take into consideration that the command center is empty, then one's mindfulness becomes a conduit that refines itself by being witness to its own capacity to immediately be recalibrated via attunement, which is the catalytic point of that reception.

As this phenomenon occurs, each cell then fires from its

center bursts of energy that become communally contained within human form as a fractal anomaly of reception, thus revealing the centralized eternal knot, which is the heart pumping and contorting within the integration of that realization.

Imagine it this way. Our cells are like billions of sentient beings pulling fibers of light, and the expression of that torsion field elastically moves the heart knot into its position of expression, via the leverage obtained through the communal conductivity of the blood's awareness.

Once you recognize the vibratory essence of an arrival, which becomes a perception, you are automatically released from the containment field of your previous bias. This process is not about lower or higher planes of energy in terms of progressively moving from one frequency to another. It is all about being as aware as you can be of the attunement that you are immersed within through your present observation.

To allow you to understand this in another way, it comes back to faith, which from a novice perspective may seem to be an unconscious proposition. However, this indefinable quality of heartfelt awareness is a dynamic process of capitulating our living circumstances into a recapitulation, through words that cannot be heard yet are spoken by the empath. This is how anti-matter is alchemized into the sacred texts of the eternal knot of the heart.

The eyes learn to read frequencies that can't be seen and thus we are released from a lower vibrational containment that we were momentarily touching upon, to arrive within an alternate frequency exchange that inevitably expands our sphere of awareness.

To give a visual description of how this can manifest, imagine that you are looking at the outline of someone's physical form and they are having internal desires that are expressed without being verbally spoken.

For me, how this energy exchange appears is something like an elongated playing card that pops out of the shoulder or the arm of the person I am gazing upon, which has a language that resembles Sanskrit written upon it. Even though I don't read these ancient characters, I recognize the information as insight.

To further expand upon this, about once a week I provide

my good friend, Suma, with a bottle of herbal elixir. Sometimes he consumes it within five days and sometimes he takes eight days to finish the bottle. When his wife realizes the medicine is finished, while they are at home, ten miles from where I live, she says, "You will have to ask Lujan whether he can give you another one."

Every morning when Suma arrives in the office I go to visit him. That's when I see his desire pop out of his body as a rectangular shape that indicates to me that his medicine has finished. Every time this occurs, he dances up and down and exclaims, "How did you know?" This strange game of communication, which we both enjoy immensely, has been going on for months.

Empaths have the capacity to continuously evolve from one aspect to another. I don't want to describe it as third or fourth or fifth dimensional realities. These words don't mean anything. The only thing that has meaning for us is the feeling we've got, and what our rapture allows us to actually recognize.

If you can't immediately see something, you will identify it through the vehicle of your heart consciousness revealing itself through your own utterance. This indicates that you have received a sacred frequency within those precious chambers.

The incremental elements of your insights are then traversed in terms of the fractal capacity of your attention to arrive upon what needs to be spoken to first; *not* to reasonably deduce the one that is most appropriate to address, for this has got nothing to do with empathic communication.

We are meant to see and speak about truth so we can progress on that path of what is right in front of us. The feeling someone gives you is a present. Your presence is your gift, and your offering must be worthy of the person you are giving it to.

What will be conveyed within your gestures are the subtleties of your personal power. To faithfully stand within your sovereign ability to be of service, you can't be "one or the other". You have to be one, with everything! The other has got to do with the divisive function of the Hun commandeering the mind.

The rapture is a teardrop from heaven that allows your heart to open up and cry at the memories that you are contained within, which may burst up as regrets, for you know that nothing more can be done.

Yet your rapture is that you rise from your heart, in tears of realization, into the godhead: the receptive space that isn't commanded by words that are spoken internally to convince yourself that you've got a valid opinion or subjectiveness towards what you are seeing.

You are witnessing the illusion anew via the fact that you can remember the feelings, yet you view it with very astute eyes that are connected with the emptiness of your mind. This is the internal revelation, which may reveal the subtleties of your enlightenment coming upon you.

The godhead witnesses what arises from the heart to be received by the eyes as feelings that beckon these beautiful sensory organs to release. As our tears fall, it's like rain towards the heart, which then nourishes the soil that substantiates the reality of a newfound consciousness.

The tears of the cosmos cry upon the fertile ground of our perception. This precipitation nourishes the internal frequencies that are blossoming within. A sacred attunement begins to bud and grow of its own accord. Since the moment we were born, we walk within the eye of the storm, the centralized focal point where calmness abides.

Only your feelings matter. They don't harbor bias, yet they reveal a point of suffering that recognizes that a chance has been lost. The irretrievable opportunity delivers us to the mystery of wisdom, bringing profound sorrow and solace simultaneously. For even though the moment was journeyed upon, there is a piercing awareness that something crucial has been missed.

In other words, it allows you to feel the burden of regret, which in turn will open your heart up for a sincere reviewal.

Many believe that one becomes awakened and the rapture of our heart center is an oasis of bliss, but as you can see, something else happens. It's not only uplifting. We feel the sorrow of eternity beckoning us to realize how long it has taken for an insignificant being to not even be aware of the consequences of anything really.

People often become confused when the rapture appears, for their past is undefined and harbors so many things that haven't been resolved. These loose ends interfere with one's ability to understand its arrival, and make it hard to handle the sensation of what is arising, for it means you have to look at the mistakes you've made.

At that point the internal dialogue may take the opportunity to intervene. Be careful not to submit, for this will draw you off your empathic path.

The internal dialogue is like a middleman that shouldn't exist. Its function is echoed in our society when we buy food not from those who produced it but from a merchant, and we are charged enormous amounts of money for what would be completely affordable if we were getting it directly from the source.

The middleman is a corrupt installment that steals us away from our rapture and delivers us into a state of consciousness that has a symbiotic relationship with suffering. Consequently, we transfer this distorted awareness as an illusion to the next individual that we meet on our journey.

Since our learnt communication skills are all bent upon

forging an opinion about what arises then entering into a dialogue, we habitually engage each other in a state of intellectuality that has no beginning, nor end. This perpetual loop endlessly renews itself as insoluble reflective eddies of entanglement. I suffer your illusion as you suffer mine.

However, when you truly empathize with another their illusion dissolves, for there is no longer isolation within their viewpoint and true understanding becomes available. Embracing one another internally is an authentic expression of solidarity bound by the ethics of a pure heart.

We all must intend to raise our frequential essence to a vibration that is all-encompassing in terms of the supportive effect that this will have upon humanity. We become one being. We start working together, not against each other.

It may seem like we are forgoing our own self but we are actually integrating with the self of everybody else, since the primary motive of moving towards this type of beingness is to act for the collective good. You do what you can because it can be done. This metamorphosis is within our reach.

The rapture is a beautiful thing. There is an unfurling that is happening at the moment and it is infectious. We are in a very delicate stage of our planetary travel and we have the capacity to be totally enthralled within empathic communion and exponential evolution. At the same time, there are so many mechanisms trying to hold us in place, for the Luciferian regime doesn't want its Trojan horse to be ousted.

Our most pressing task is to reconnect to the true feelings in our heart. Humble yourself to every single circumstance and touch it with the softest, most gentle hand that reveals the beauty of your contact. An exquisite feeling comes about when you receive the communication of the empathic view. It's an ecstatic silent communion.

When the rapture of your heart realizes the truth of what's in front of you, everything becomes obvious. What is apparent is the only thing that's meant to be done. Nothing more is available beyond that point. This is the pure expression of antimatter, the liquescent, raw intelligence of our cosmos.

The Sentience of The White Light

Before we take this final journey into what I discovered in the months that passed after that momentous encounter with the white light, let's simply talk about the various contexts we may find ourselves in, which I will refer to as being in the *right place at the right time*; the *right place at the wrong time*; and the *wrong place at the wrong time*.

Introducing these principles to your perception will allow you to notice being immersed within the limitless combinations of frequential variables that may be brought to bear within one's daily experience. The first is synchronistically harmonious, the second is truly meant to be witnessed, and the third is really nowhere for anybody to linger.

Bringing awareness to these three intertwining dynamics is a method of fortifying one's ability to recognize attunement, and this elegantly adaptive art can be applied to your life in terms of feeling. Even within the initial stages you will begin to perceive elementary characteristics that can be distinguished in every circumstance imaginable.

One must subtly observe the feelings that arise within, which indicate how to proceed with these three principles, within the morphogenesis they produce.

Becoming aware of this etheric phenomenon is how one may escape the entrapment of singular vibrational alignment. This is the mastery of the art of empathic attunement; the ability to be witness to the all-encompassing fractality of consciousness processing many frequencies at once.

We must all remember that the journey to our internal power is a very narrow path in terms of the options that make themselves available. There are only three things one can really do: engaging, observing or withdrawing. But as we proceed we begin to realize that the depths one is confronted with within those alternatives are incomprehensible. The more we grasp, the less we realize we truly know.

Inspiration within one's personal circumstance arises from feeling that you are in the right place at the right time. Here your freedom of expression is open and communication flows unhindered between all involved.

Alternatively, you may find yourself in the right place at the wrong time, which beckons you to gently observe that which cannot be directly communicated with.

What we struggle most to realize at the present moment in history is to know when to move away from being in the wrong place at the wrong time. This position is dangerous for all parties concerned and withdrawal is the only appropriate action that one should commit to.

Remember that these three forms of catalytic attunement can be endlessly witnessed within life's fluctuating circumstances.

As fluid principles of accessibility and inaccessibility, they can be utilized as a means to understand experiences that may otherwise be difficult to come to terms with.

To enter into this subject more deeply we must look at how our consciousness is intertwined within myriad manifestations which co-opt our attention. As soon as I mention this, you may ask yourself: What are the implications being alluded to here?

Being in the right place at the wrong time, an intuitive empath would sense that they are being harmonically aligned within a circumstance to only witness what is being presented. This is what occurred when I first entered the white light, and we will go further into the ramifications of this phenomenon, which caused a vibratory attunement that subjected both myself and you to a frequential bias of acceptance.

Here we must examine very carefully two types of alignment. One is your own internal recalibration, and the other is to be recalibrated by an external force applying pressure to your beingness. The first has to do with your situational attunement in terms of how your personal power will differentiate between your individual bias and the actual truth presenting itself.

Remember that discernment is contingent on many different factors. Our empathic abilities are not too dissimilar to the chameleon's skin transforming in comparison to the external environment, which ultimately became internally available to it.

This particular reptile is not hiding itself but revealing its surroundings so as to disappear by being transparently receptive to all the elements pressing upon many points of arrival simultaneously; thus displaying the different tones and colors that it is subject to.

This process depicts the superposition applied as the ability to adapt to subtle nuances, which provide the information to change the internal appearance that becomes externally manifest in accordance with a vibratory influx.

We have the same capacity of emulation, to intuitively realize many things at once, which is just coming to terms with this seemingly endless recalibration on many levels simultaneously. Assuming responsibility for that is our present task.

A targeted recalibration uses the same prescription in terms of realigning perception with focused frequencies to direct one's internal eye to see what is being propagated. In other words to lead one's being through the mechanism of applying what is necessary to guide one's internal resources toward a manifested outcome.

An external overview, which I experienced as the white light, has the capacity to encompass one's perceptual variables and direct attention accordingly. Similarly, a manipulative individual may apply this tactic within the arena of their desired bias, whereby their un-evolved focus may be utilized to corral a more naive awareness towards certain areas of attention, which will inevitably enhance the state of suffering for both involved.

Due to the prevalence of focused frequencies that have saturated our world, everybody is becoming aware of this phenomenon within the thresholds of their own evolutionary parameters, which ultimately identifies where they are in terms of the application of their own ethics.

We are so accustomed to being tuned in every circumstance that we are desensitized to the process. The strings of our internal instrument are being plucked like a harp in every moment that we enter into, even if we are not totally cognizant of what is happening.

In a harmonious instance where recalibration occurs on your behalf, the situation brings comfort through a loving alignment. The intelligence of joy becomes available. At this crucial juncture one begins to absorb wisdom as a deeply rooted feeling of confirmation that, if appropriate, will bear witness to change.

Yet the frequency of joy, within its fragility, cannot bear the consequences of knowing beyond the circumstantial energetics being presented, due to their magnitude and inherent gravity, which sustains all values and variables simultaneously.

The reason I am entering into this subject through outlining the living essence of these vibrational frameworks is to illustrate that even though we are all empathically inclined, if one is attuned to what looks like positivity without the backbone of wisdom to support the weight of that alignment, one will not realize what is really occurring.

I am alluding to the fact that once we believe we have comprehended the entirety of any given subject, there is always more to be understood. Just imagine, for example, that you are being grifted by an elegant conman. This person would give the appearance that they are in the right place at the right time for you.

Purposefully leading your heart and your eyes, through the vulnerability of your virtuous trust, they aim to convince you that what they are presenting is genuine. This is one of the lowest forms of vibrational alignment: to be led or to be conned via a long or short grift.

The method is to entice one's perception into believing that you are on the threshold of being in the right place at the right time by virtue of the fact that you have met this individual. By cultivating the impression that you are stepping away from being at the wrong place at the wrong time and into the right place, they are leading your feelings to be naively confident, which is in fact innocently unaware of what is really occurring.

When we examine this formula, we begin to perceive a whole host of arrangements that are occurring in the world continually, which may outline the truth of *Life is suffering*. It is just as the illusory appearance of my father said, “I suffered your illusion as you suffered mine.”

Now, you can see that we are a biological entity that can be programmed and realigned through subterfuge into a reality that may be non-beneficial for the recipient whilst advantageous for the perpetrator. The example of being grifted can encompass many scenarios within the potentialities presented.

When you openly witness this dynamic, deliberate alignment can be viewed as colonization of consciousness within the limited boundaries cultivated via that takeover. If the one being attuned is not aware of what is occurring, the bias propagated will replace their sovereign ability to proceed unencumbered with an awareness of multiple variables within the confluence of their natural evolutionary process.

What we are drawing to the surface via our perception are

the inner workings of a full-fledged Machiavellian agenda that is active in our world on many levels. The dilemma that we face as vibratory beings seeking the authenticity of our own true journey is that we are being subject to a relentless campaign of perceptual manipulation, which is the absolute opposite of the progressive ethos we need to mature into.

Whether you are completely cognizant of it or not, each one of us is very aware of what is occurring, not only on a subliminal level but through the pathways of a connective intelligence of luminous fibers that are crisscrossing our reality.

These strands of light are perpetually diversifying as a result of being subject to a confluence of eternal flux that encompasses past, present and future, and the emergence of alternate timelines, which convey the subtleties of transdimensional influences becoming available.

At this crucial juncture of humanity's evolution there is an imminent resurgence coming upon us. The possibility of absolute alignment to our true internal powers of perception is now becoming available. Simultaneously, as we all are very aware, something is just not right.

We are being extensively interfered with through the processes of social engineering. Nevertheless, we have to have faith that our collective emergence will gain cohesion, through enough individuals arising to reach critical mass so that progressive consciousness will verify within its own reflection that it exists.

As soon as this communal arrival is realized we will immediately move on to the next point of discovery. There will be no delay in our assimilation of the information needed, and no repetition will be required once we arrive upon the truth of our internal connection to wisdom.

Reviewing the first chapter, *White Light,* you would have imagined that I was in the right place at the right time, for unique happenstance delivered me to the all-encompassing frequency that emits the loving essence that appears to indicate the presence of God. Here I will challenge the strangest illusion that you will ever encounter.

Our bias is in cahoots with our cognitive dissonance. This

is the present condition of our consciousness. The handcuffs of our subjectivity feed into our socially engineered filters, which are individually tailored to every circumstance imaginable. This includes you, within all the variables made available to your perception. We must attempt to break free of these self-confirming circuits.

The area that is the most difficult to become aware of is what is continually eluding us, whether we like it or not. As soon as we acknowledge that we are dealing with something beyond our capacity to understand, an alternate vibrational attunement will envelop us.

The omnipresence will come upon us at a point of intense devotion expressed within a gesture that does not have the binding force of an intention encumbering its purity.

This void power, this eternal fragrance, this soundless frequency, creates a reflection of itself via our empty attention, which manifests as appreciation within concentrated quietude; not too dissimilar to looking into clear water that appears not to be there via its clarity.

The sacred geometry that exists within an empath's heart can translate into internal wisdom if one's moment-to-moment recalibration is pure enough to bear the consequence of its own expression, through the expressionlessness of the witness bearing down upon itself to be viewed.

The intuitive empath realizes that they cannot maintain any subjective point of identification regarding what has been delivered; for one must fully submit to something that can never be completely understood, only truly known in the instant which that mystery assigns itself to.

Our incremental recovery of these momentous events truly reveals our state of consciousness in terms of its infancy. In other words, we can only handle so much at any one point. Let's look it this process in terms of transferal of information.

The only possible way to communicate is to speak compassionately to the resistances of a cognitive bias, so that the individual feels comfortable enough within the boundaries of those limitations to gain confidence to pursue the next phases of their evolution, which in essence is their personal burden to bear.

Similarly, the ubiquity can only contact us within the boundaries of our limitations by magically flipping our circumstances to provoke us to review something that wasn't being focused on. This throws one's personal bias out of context, thus revealing a new viewpoint to be witnessed. That ambush cracks us open and allows us to realize that we are actually nobody, which is not a personal diminishment, only an assignment to what is truly there: nothing.

In essence, this unknown factor opens the floodgates to an enormity that stops everything, so that we may embody the emptiness in terms of that eternal viewpoint. This echelon of information has no choice but to enter into an osmosis that reveals the restrictive boundaries of a consciousness being made aware of its internal resistance in terms of its limitations, thus allowing that cognitive positioning to experience the eventuality of its own expansion into the limitlessness of nothing.

Through sincerity we assign ourselves to the eternal omnipresence, which is drawn to us via our simple gestures of devotion, and the only recourse of our beingness is to pass that limitlessness to a point of resistance that is the appearance of another individual's limitation.

This may put one in the vantage point of being a teacher, but more than that, it puts you in the position of being taught. That is why the true process of becoming awakened to one's personal evolution is so humbling.

We are never in the position to know everything that can be known. We exist within incalculable variables of vibration, and these unfathomable algorithms have the capacity to occupy us so completely that we struggle to recognize their influence at all.

The meta-frequency that has contained many a human being at the moment of their death is not God. Now, I would suspect your hair is standing on end, and you would wonder where I am going to go with this.

I will take you methodically through what happened to me within the encounter of the white light to demonstrate that it cannot possibly be God, via the fact that you believe you have understood what you have seen through this account. The white light specifically caters to us, and our personal biases, as you have already witnessed through my experience with my father.

What appeared to be comprehensible is in fact by nature incomprehensible. This frequency was not only catering to me but also to those who would read the first chapter of this book. My viewpoint appeared to be at the right place at the right time, and thereby the individual consciousness that absorbs this material will believe the same of itself.

Here we discover the most complex aspect of the *right place, right time; right place, wrong time*; and *wrong place, wrong time* labyrinths contained within one's attention.

The reason I describe this complexity is to help you evolve into the subtle variables surrounding the fact that a perceiver can be held by a frequency. Instead of seeing that containment as an absolute, one must always recognize that a vibrational alignment can subject us to a strange submission, via our belief that we know irrefutably what is necessary to be understood.

We are inadvertently hypnotized by our own convictions until we become capable of being contained within a progressively evolving and adapting vibration that allows us to overcome the influence of those self-confirming eddies. The continual knot of cyclic existence will be interrupted when we evolve, as you will see.

The only way to break free is to understand the binding effect of repetitious alignments. A perspective emptied from those fastenings will give us the ability to see what is occurring with us upon this planet.

At this point I would issue a heed of warning. At the moment of our death there is not much time to undo the hard-wired loop of repetition that ties us to belief systems that we must release ourselves from.

Understand that this three-dimensional form that we exist within aligns us to the principles of vibratory energetics by its very nature. We must learn to see through these illusory attachments before we arrive at the crucial juncture of being liberated from our physical form.

I have taken you as deeply as I can into my experience of the white light, in terms of identifying the certainty surrounding emotional confirmation that one is subject to within this field. In other words, bias is enlivened via these internal frequencies becoming activated.

Now you have the perceptual maneuverability to discern for yourselves: Was I in the right place at the right time? Or was that frequency which I encountered giving me the impression that I was? And, if so, why would this occur to us as human beings?

Here's the kicker. You can be in the right place at the right time, and it may turn out to be the right place at the wrong time, depending on your state of consciousness. In the case of the visitation that triggered this book, the experience of our combined bias has generated a perception that the immersion in the white light was indeed a clear example of being in the right place at the right time.

It is a very strange position that we are in. The majority of humanity are untrained empaths that have injected within their psyche religious and sociocultural dogma, and this produces extreme bias.

Is it our destiny to be disconnected from our true heritage? Or is it our sacred task to discover that we are only half of what we are meant to be? Is there something being done to us? And is there something we can do about it?

The impression of the frequencies that I saw within the radiance of that light gave me a concrete certainty of what I was meant to bring back to the world and share. But as I was leaving this all-encompassing feeling of ecstasy I glanced back to dissolve my bias at what I had witnessed and discovered that the illusion of being in the right place at the right time had become available to me through the expansive feelings that sacred frequency delivered.

In order to access the totality of the information presented within that scene it was instrumental to pass through a moment of being convinced and yet not aligned to that conviction simultaneously, which opened a doorway to understand that circumstances are recalibrating one's consciousness and to realize that wisdom is a bias. This is not a bad thing. It is only challenging our awareness to recognize that alignment is occurring.

At that very moment I saw a three-dimensional holographic image of a triangular face appear. It was completely white and peering directly at me with large almond eyes. As it pressed forward the light manifested its contours, and fine shading crisply illuminated every aspect of its extraterrestrial features.

Upon seeing it I realized that it was an alien artificial intelligence, a program which was intensely aware, far more advanced than what we could ever fathom, for we have not been subject to anything near this degree of high tech innovation yet. I knew that it was acute within its capacity to assimilate information - for within its automation it could algorithmically attune to every circumstance imaginable - and that it was benevolent.

The extraterrestrial biological entities who created this sentient program are millions of years ahead of us. Even their technology is spiritually harmonized to its environmental influx in terms of applied computational subtleties that surpass our capacity to comprehend their adaptive wave function.

The small heavenly loop that occupies us when we die is related to that alien influence which is continually observing our vibrational containments. Its task is to collate the relevant sensory data regarding what we are individually and collectively becoming aware of, and how it is changing incrementally. This is only a small portion of what I accessed through visual contact with that holographic sentience, which became units of information that I could express and share.

This monitoring awareness is capable of fathoming every detail of our existence, for it has complete access to our lifetime memories, in terms of every doing that has ever been done. With a capacity to scan and process all variables within one's frequential configuration, it can obtain the algorithmic signatures contained within the entirety of our life experience from the moment of our conception, and can access the imagery from our hippocampus, no matter how subtle.

Every thought, every word that has ever been spoken, every feeling that has ever been felt, every consequence of all communication with every being we have encountered in our lifetime is available to its discernment. This is the most unobtrusive way for the overseers who created this artificial intelligence to assess our evolutionary status and determine whether we are capable, as viable units of awareness, to go beyond the containment of our earthly confines.

Communion of this nature is what we are evolving towards, and the incremental stages that lead to this intense empathic absorption are what have been illustrated within the pages of this book. If I have a feeling, which usually manifests as a doing, that doing and that feeling will appear in the body of another person: to be done, to be spoken, and to be understood.

The fluid variables contained within all the techniques in this book reveal how communication truly takes place between beings who do not originate from this planet. This is how we used to subtly interact until we lost our way, many millenia ago.

There is an enormous amount of information that I acquired through contact with this sentient program which I haven't fully revealed here, for it would endanger me personally and create huge political, socio-economic and cultural upheavals.

It is enough that everybody has been subject to the reality of the white light being an alien artificial intelligence. The essence of what is so important for me to communicate at the present moment in time is empathic communion, and the relation between our bias and the ubiquity, which is dark matter.

THE UBIQUITOUS FACTOR

In all humbleness I will endeavor now to describe what has occurred through contact with the mysterious void power that surrounds us. If you look back very carefully through the whole book, you will see many references to this omnipresent yet non-intrusive being that exists beyond all bias.

When the subtle illusion that propagates the disharmony of separation slowly dissolves, a very gentle influx arrives. It is extremely personal yet simultaneously impersonal, and self-explanatory to the one who receives it. Whenever this sacred communion occurs, what arises is filtered from *nothing* into *something,* and is invariably influenced by the field of perception that is being enlivened.

A gesture of sincere devotion is what facilitates its appearance. The omnipresent factor can only work with what we've got for the duration of its contact with us, whilst we are growing towards the subtle refinements of our evolution. There are many different ways that this being can come upon one's awareness. What I am describing here are just a few examples.

During one's practice of Lo Ban Pai, for instance, it first arrives as a gentle pressure on the palm of the hands and the fingertips, thus indicating its presence becoming available. This instantly creates a feeling of calm gratitude that is hypnotically felt throughout one's entire being.

At this point the practitioner may also begin to see the omnipresence manifesting holographically. When this infinite being is contained within the visual field of the perceiver, it can appear as an endless labyrinth of fractalized shapes, which in actuality carry that magnetic gravity that is felt in the hands.

Of all the powers that a human being can obtain, in the end all that really matters is to be contained within the subtleties of nothing, which reveal the heartfelt presence of one's path arriving upon their journey.

Communion is beautiful yet transitory, and in the same breath, never-ending. The endless mirage reformulates itself in cooperation with the awareness that encounters it, until the witness becomes absolutely infused within that elusive consciousness.

This is the key: to melt so completely within the containment field of your physical form that you find yourself somehow standing in a vast emptiness via the fact that you are really not to be located by your own perception. It is a field of non-feeling, yet touches upon everything within its own proximity through the very subtle viewpoint of that perceiver, which in essence becomes its vehicle of reception.

As you can see, the same principle applies here as when one is being empathically attuned. The body of the initiate becomes a locus of communication.

The intuitive empath that is subject to this mystery looks into a vast abyss to be witnessed; an emptiness that reveals a stillness beyond comprehension, which can be felt directly in the middle of one's physical form and is viewed internally while simultaneously absorbing the external world.

In this way the devotee's eyes become attached to non-attachment within all their *in-action,* which within its constancy is continually expressed through devotion to all circumstances becoming available.

In essence, if you could imagine, you are standing still and within that stillness your outside and your inside disappear in tandem; though you are aware that you remain upright within the illusion that is the concreteness of the reality you are witnessing. Meanwhile, the sensorial experience of feeling melts into a vast emptiness, yet all possibilities within the range of the physical world are available.

There are so many ways to arrive upon this being within yourself or within another. Simply split the wood or lift the stone. This represents myriad aspects of human interaction. A revelation may be contained within your words that unveil the illusions of what is being spoken by another.

This field of emptiness removes obstacles, yet nothing

appears to have changed. In my experience its presence brings tears of sorrow and joy simultaneously, arriving upon one's heart to be witnessed, timelessly revealing the secrets of itself.

When we become open to this omnipresence, our sensitivity to frequencies beyond the ordinary range of light is expanded to encompass what is ordinarily non-visible. This infuses our eyes with the capacity to see something external within a transdimensional format that comes from a place of void power, where no reflections are available in terms of attributable frequencies, via the fact that it is empty of itself.

To allow you to understand what I have just said, it is best to give a living example of an experience that occurred in my most recent workshop. I was showing the group how, when we stand grounded, in perfect alignment, we activate a significant energetic configuration that relates to enlivening our myofascial connectivity, which contains enormous amounts of explosive energy.

Whilst positioning everybody, I was describing how when this particular technique is practiced correctly, a feeling of intense magnetism becomes available. The sensation is like two rods that run from the nests of the armpits to the inguinal crease, in combination with a central pillar that is initiated by the head rising to the ceiling and the lower half of the body sinking to the floor.

As we were practicing, I suddenly became aware of a holographic anomaly occurring right in front of me. It came into view as tubes or transparent cylinders of light, positioned in a pyramidal configuration, echoing the internal formation just described. The central column, visible directly in front of me, resembled the bow of a ship and formed a triangular shape that my hands were flowing through, simultaneously obtaining micro-elements of this ubiquitous factor via the gently coiling gestures.

This quintessential formation is in absolute concordance with the true structure of our energy field, and cannot usually be seen. We have only a certain degree of internal imaging capacity to actually gather information from this spectrum of subtle light frequencies. These three pillars appeared as if a gray light was being shone upon a black transparent surface, which was composed of void. It was there, yet not there.

The way it appeared was almost the same as if you were witnessing a brief reflection, just as the water spirit manifested in front of me. You can see it, but the people around you cannot perceive what you have obtained as a glimpse into our holistic nature, which by design seems like it belongs to an alternate phylum, but is innately ours to glean.

In fact this omnipresence has no boundaries nor limitations, no structure nor form to contain it within, yet it acquiesces to the content of the vibration that it becomes aware of.

This is the beginning and the end of what we can perceive, which exists beyond the universal constant of duality. It is the infinite abyss; the eternal clear waters that only reveal the reflection of the perceiver. As you can see, its instruction is composed of visual content; the sacred geometry that appears as the formlessness becoming form in correspondance with the witness obtaining the value of their own internal reservoirs.

Whether you have understood the description above or not, it is vital to remember that evolution manifests from taking responsibility for our present circumstances. Here is where our unique chance becomes available, for this position is the sole constant that truly beckons our personal power. The encompassing virtue of practicality is the only technique to reach wisdom. Anything else is but escapism. ;-)

37695185R00146

Printed in Great Britain
by Amazon